You Can Say NO to Your Teenager

You Can Say NO to Your Teenager

And Other Strategies for Effective Parenting in the 1990s

Jeanette Shalov, M.S.
Irwin Sollinger, Ph.D.
Jules Spotts, Ph.D.
Phyllis S. Steinbrecher, M.A.
Douglas W. Thorpe, M.S.

▲▼ ADDISON-WESLEY PUBLISHING COMPANY, INC.

Reading, Massachusetts • Menlo Park, California • New York
Don Mills, Ontario • Wokingham, England • Amsterdam • Bonn
Sydney • Singapore • Tokyo • Madrid • San Juan
Paris • Seoul • Milan • Mexico City • Taipei

LIBRARY OF CONGRESS CATALOGING-IN-PUBLICATION DATA

YOU CAN SAY NO TO YOUR TEENAGER : AND OTHER STRATEGIES FOR
    EFFECTIVE PARENTING IN THE 1990S / BY JEANETTE SHALOV . . . [ET AL.].
       P. CM.
     INCLUDES INDEX.
     ISBN 0-201-57002-5
     ISBN 0-201-60826-X (PBK.)
     1. TEENAGERS—UNITED STATES.   2. PARENTING—UNITED STATES.
    3. ADOLESCENT PSYCHOLOGY—UNITED STATES.   I. SHALOV, JEANETTE.
    HQ796.Y578   1991
   649'.125—DC20   90-41388
                                                          CIP

COVER DESIGN BY HANNUS DESIGN ASSOCIATES
TEXT DESIGN BY MELINDA GROSSER FOR *silk*
SET IN 11-POINT GARAMOND BY ST ASSOCIATES, WAKEFIELD, MA.

123456789-MW-9695949392
FIRST PRINTING, DECEMBER 1990
FIRST PAPERBACK PRINTING, FEBRUARY 1992

Next Stages is deeply indebted to the families with whom we have worked over the years. Their courage as they faced the problematic issues of their lives has given us insight and the ability to look upon our own struggles.

With this in mind we would like to dedicate this book to our children and families. They have endured living with us and have made the journey of reaching the next stage worthwhile and meaningful.

The trouble with the kitten is that
Eventually it becomes a cat.
Ogden Nash

Contents

Acknowledgments

The work of Next Stages began with workshops held in Connecticut at the New Canaan Country School in New Canaan and at Coleytown Middle School in Westport. The parents, teachers, and administrators who attended these sessions were of enormous assistance in framing the issues of this book. In particular, Nicholas Thacher, headmaster of the New Canaan Country School and Dr. Daniel Christianson of Coleytown Middle School were strategic and challenging with comments and suggestions.

Martha Moutray, senior editor at Addison-Wesley, proved enormously helpful, with her editing prowess and her guidance.

And Dan Woog was a pivotal guide and helper throughout the preparation and completion of this book. He began the task as a co-worker and ended the project as a friend.

1 | **W**elcome to Parenting: Now You're a POA

The door slams; the untied sneakers thud along the kitchen floor. The refrigerator is opened, and for a long, long time the door remains ajar.

"Hi, dear. How was school?" you ask.

"I can't believe we never have anything decent to eat in this place," he replies.

Your adolescent is home.

"How was school?" you persevere.

There is a long, food-driven pause. "I'm going to a party at Rick's tonight," he finally announces. You had been steeling yourself to remind him to please put the cereal back where he found it, but this latest bit of news demands a quick, if measured, response.

"Well, I don't know. Are his parents going to be there?"

The mumbled answer lies somewhere on the continuum between "mm-hmm" and "uh-uh"; his eyes are nowhere to be seen. Despite the danger signs lighting up in every corner of your brain, you do something you intensely hate to do: You repeat the question.

"I said, are his parents going to be there?"

"I don't know. How should I know?" is the reply, a study in pained exasperation. Then, a sudden downshift to anger. "Who cares? What are you so worried about, anyway? Everybody's going. All their parents said yeah."

Signaling reluctance, hoping to buy time while you plan your counteroffensive, you venture a tentative, "Well honey, I'm not sure . . ."

"Oh my God, I can't believe you," he erupts, disgust dripping from every syllable. "You're so old-fashioned, it's . . . it's unbelievable. Just because you never went to any parties when you were a kid . . ."

You pause a moment, then place what seems to be a reasonable suggestion on the table. "Well, can I at least call Rick's mother to see . . ."

He knows what's coming, and isn't about to hear it. Abruptly, he cuts you off: "No. No way! *No way!* Don't you *dare* call Rick's mom. Don't call *anybody!*"

Barely missing a beat, he moves into his martyr mode. "You're the one who's always saying my friends should come over more. Why d'you think they don't, huh, Mom? Nobody else has to put up with this third degree." Then the zinger: "If you don't let me go, it'll be *your* fault nobody likes me."

You're helpless before this verbal onslaught, this witch's brew of wrath, petulance, pleading, and insecurity. You don't know what to say—but he knows, precisely.

"I can't believe you. I can't believe you don't trust me."

A pause for dramatic effect. "Thanks a lot. Thanks a *real lot*, Mom."

That does it. You've got some power yourself, some leverage over this kid, and now you're determined to use it.

"If you can't live in this house, young man . . . ." you threaten, suddenly clueless as to what "then" should follow your precipitous "if."

"Fine," he counters, ending the argument on his own terms. "Fine. Then I won't live in this house." And off he storms, up to his room, where he slams the door, stomps around for a while, then rams the least musically palatable CD he can find into his sound system. And cranks it up to jackhammer level.

You're still debating the proper response to the party debacle when suddenly you've got this music issue to deal with too.

Welcome to adolescence—or, more precisely, to the parent-of-adolescent experience.

How did this happen? How did you reach this battlefield, this emotional war zone in which danger lurks in every direction you turn? Look one way, and there's a skirmish over fads or fashions; look another, and it's a confrontation about alcohol or drugs. Take one step forward and you're fighting over sexuality; one step back, and the tangle involves family and friends. And whichever way you travel, you know there's no turning back.

What's especially disturbing is that just a few minutes ago, or so it seems, you and your child were strolling hand in hand down the path toward maturity. You shared jokes, confidences, precious time; your lives were intertwined, and parenting was a joy. Suddenly, virtually without warning, your cute little preadolescent has metamorphosed into a surly, moody, challenging, independent, manipulative know-it-all. And that's on a good day.

How did this happen? How did this child turn up in your loving, caring, supportive family? Was it something you yourself did or said—or did *not* do or say—that caused this instantaneous transformation to take place, before your very own eyes and under your very own roof?

And, you wonder, if your son is acting like this today, what's he going to be like a week, a month, a year from now? How do you feel about the changes that are taking place in his mind, his body, his life? And, more important, what can you do about them?

It is important to recognize that adolescence is a time of growth. In fact, the root of the Latin word *adolescere*, meaning "to grow up," is the same as the root for the word "adult." An adolescent is a child who is in the act of *growing into* an adult. However, that growth process involves a myriad of annoying, perplexing, and frightening behavior patterns, including (but unfortunately not limited to) lack of impulse control, the need for instant gratification, identity confusion, a desire for separation and independence, challenge to authority, limit-testing, movement away from parents toward peer groups for support, sexual experimentation, substance experimentation, mood swings, and physical and intellectual development of enormous proportions.

At the same time, *you* are also growing into a new role: parent of adolescent (or "POA"). And as part of that growth process you feel shock, disappointment, guilt, confusion, competition, resentment, exasperation, jealousy, desertion, fear, challenge, and even sexual tension.

This growth process may also trigger painful memories from your own adolescence. Images like waiting for weeks for a prom invitation that never came, being cut from a sports team all your friends made, or being shorter (or taller, fatter, thinner, hairier, or less hairy) than every other boy or girl in your class may resurface without warning, nearly as sharp as they were two or three decades ago, when they were experiences you were sure you would never survive.

Not a bit like toilet training or the first swimming lesson, is it?

Adolescence has been compared to giving birth to a new child. Parents feel the same pain, excitement, and limitless potential they felt the first time they set eyes on their newborn baby—but this time they can't expect quick results, or glory in wondrous accomplishments. Such milestones as the first smile, the first recognition of familiar faces, and the first faltering steps are long past, replaced now by the first fight over choice of friends, the first automobile accident, the first evening when you're not exactly sure where your child is.

Gone, too, are the days when the power structure within your family was clearly delineated: You had it, and your kids didn't. As a POA, your power to enforce rules and regulations is no longer singular; your command "Get ready, we're leaving in ten minutes" is not met with compliance, but with a defiant "I'm not going."

Adolescence is a tremendous opportunity, a beautiful chance for children to be reassembled—largely by themselves—into real, honest-to-goodness decent adult human beings. Adolescents have been doing this for years—you did it yourself—but when it's happening, it's nearly impossible for parents to recognize that this process of reassembly can actually work.

It takes a gigantic act of faith on your part to believe that somehow one day you will receive a return on your investment. It takes great effort and perception to recognize that a critical issue of adolescence is not ceding power to your child, but rather developing parenting skills that will help him gain power over his own life.

And it takes an enormous amount of parental self-esteem to know that this adolescent—this rebellious, awkward, cantankerous person who, though physically and intellectually employable, not only acts unemployable but gives every indication he'll remain so for the rest of his life—will one day, in the not-too-distant (yet, unfortunately, also not-too-near) future, bridge that enormous chasm between your expectations of him, and the reality of his daily actions.

But it will happen. As long as adolescents have existed, they eventually have grown into adults, as yours will too.

The tasks of parenting in the '90s are the same as they always have been: providing enough stability while encouraging enough independence to allow an adolescent to grow up relatively healthy, possibly wealthy, and at least moderately wise. However, the challenges of this new decade are far different from those faced by any earlier generation of parents.

As a result, parents of the '90s must confront adolescents and the world around them in a unique way. Changing demographics, the surge in single-parent families and households in which both parents work outside the home, society's ever-increasing emphasis on "success" (as measured by fast cars, expensive clothes, and admission to the "right" college), the twin specters of AIDS and crack (along with a host of other sexually transmitted diseases and dangerous drugs)—these and countless other factors will have very real, and in most cases negative, effects on the adolescent experience of the '90s.

Many of you POAs now reading this book went through your own adolescence during a decade legendary for its turbulence. You came of age at a time when traditional values were being put to stern tests. The concepts and precepts your own parents grew up with were not the ideas and ideals you embraced; you had to find your own way, charting an often hazardous course between the extremes of autocracy and permissiveness. For better or worse, the '90s promise to be a decade filled with similar strife—only this time, the challenges and demands of parenthood will be even more difficult.

The good news is you can meet those challenges and face those demands. You can create an atmosphere in your home and in your daily interactions with your adolescent that will not only lead to but even actively encourage positive growth.

That atmosphere can be created in as many different ways as there are families with adolescents, including single-parent families and blended families as well as two-parent families. In the end, though, all those ways share one common element: a parent or parents with the courage to say no.

By learning how to say no in appropriate situations, and in your own personal words and style, you will take a giant step toward lessening the tensions that pervade life with adolescents; you will contribute mightily toward your adolescent's development as a responsible, contributing member of society—and you will do so while maintaining your own self-esteem, sense of humor, and feeling of family leadership. In short, learning how to say no to your adolescent will enable you to survive your adolescent's adolescence, and your own parent-of-adolescent experience.

Consider these two scenarios.

Stacy, a licensed driver for three weeks, wants to drive her date to the Evergreen Ball and then to a wee-hours party in a neighboring town. Filled with trepidation, her parents agree to lend her the car. When the January evening becomes foggy and rainy, their doubts increase, but because they feel it is important to show Stacy that they trust her they don't ask her to make alternate plans.

Fifteen minutes after Stacy drives out the driveway, the car is totaled.

In spite of their very valid concerns—about the weather, their daughter's driving experience, the combination of a formal dance and an early morning party—Stacy's parents choose the expedient route. Instead of voicing their worries, facing up to the fragility of their relationship with this new young driver in their midst, and seeking alternatives with Stacy and her friends, they avoid conflict. Fortunately, they manage to avoid a major disaster, but they do end up buying a new car far earlier than they had planned.

The second example involves an evening just as fraught with danger as a formal dance or graduation night. David, a high school senior, and his friends have been looking forward to New Year's Eve for weeks. He informs his parents that he plans to host a small party, and to avoid trouble, he'll serve as "keymaster" (keeper of the car keys). When his parents try to dissuade him tactfully, he snaps at them. "What do you want us to do instead? Stand around on some dead-end street and drink?"

So David's parents discuss New Year's Eve—first between themselves, then with their son—and eventually they agree to the party and settle upon some ground rules. The party must be indoors; it must be over by 1 A.M., and once the guests arrive, absolutely no one is to leave.

According to David, that creates consternation in his gang. "You're ruining New Year's Eve!" he cries. But because the notion of a cold evening covertly celebrating in a few parked cars is less appealing to them than a night spent by a warm fire, they agree to the restrictions.

And they end up having a wonderful time. Although they might not realize it, they accept the structure David's parents impose and turn it into an enjoyable party. There is a minimal amount of drinking—they don't feel any pressure to "get trashed"—and end up dancing, talking, even playing board games most of the night.

As part of their agreement, David's parents call before returning home. When they walk in the door, they find a nearly spotless home and a houseful of happy teenagers, with whom they spend the next couple of hours chatting.

Like Stacy's parents, David's say yes—to the party—but unlike Stacy's they also say no—to impulsive, potentially ominous behavior. But they say no creatively, caringly, and carefully, and that makes all the difference.

Of course, learning how to say no—appropriately, clearly, lovingly—is no easy task. You already know that, simply by observing the seemingly random behavior your adolescent exhibits day after puzzling day.

Throughout his entire life, his growth in every realm—physical, intellectual, emotional—has been measured inch by inch and pound by pound in joyful, incremental steps. Every week he added new words to his vocabulary; with each year he showed a growing understanding of, and commitment to, our planet. Then on that fateful day, he boarded the wild roller coaster ride in the amusement park we call adolescence.

Overnight, his behavior has turned random. On Monday he bounds around the house making gorilla noises; on Tuesday you and he hold a deep, soul-satisfying discussion about the heroism of Anne Frank; on Wednesday he's back imitating an ape.

What is important to understand is this: There is no randomness to adolescent behavior, no matter how capricious it may seem. Every bit of behavior your adolescent visits upon you has meaning. Granted, he may not be aware of that meaning (nor may you, for that matter), but before you can say no to your adolescent, you must realize that all his actions—every word he speaks, every sneer he sneers, every costume he dons—means something.

For example, your adolescent's rational, articulate ideas about Anne Frank might be his way of saying, "I feel like an adult. I am mature, I am wise, I am in full control of my reasoning and my intellect." His simian behavior might mean, "Sometimes I also feel like a child. I am not yet grown up, and I can't always control my impulses."

It is crucial for you as a parent of an adolescent to recognize that this behavior is not random; like all adolescent behavior, it has meaning. But, even beyond that, you must realize that this behavior is not directed *at* you; rather, it is a symbolic way for your adolescent to express feelings. You must learn how to decipher the meaning of the behavior and figure out what action you should take based on that meaning, rather than simply respond to the behavior itself. It's the difference between feeling, "Boy, my kid's being a real pain to me," and thinking, "Wow, what a strange way for her to act. I wonder what that means to her."

Or to explain it another way, it's like the difference between two types of leg movements: the involuntary jerk that results when the doctor smacks your knee with a reflex hammer, and the calculated leap that enables you to deftly avoid a puddle and land, completely dry, on the other side.

This advice—to strive for action, not reaction—is no doubt easier for us to give than it is for you to learn. This book can at least help you discover the strategies to find your own method of accomplishing this goal. A couple of additional examples may help clarify the distinction between action and reaction—between responding to annoying behavior that appears aimed at you and taking one step back and asking, "What is she trying to say to me?" These examples may clarify the difference between focusing on one single event that occurs at one specific moment in time, and understanding the broad implication that event has for you and your adolescent.

After several phone calls and letters, and the trading of a few favors, you finally have wangled tickets for the entire family to attend the much-publicized King Tut exhibit when it comes to the city. You've planned a big day: After viewing the exhibit and exploring other exhibits in the museum, you're meeting your old college roommate for dinner. He's bringing his wife and son, Lance, who at sixteen is exactly the same age as your daughter, Debbi.

You fight the traffic and the crowds—and suddenly find yourself face-to-face with King Tut, in all his 3000-year-old golden splendor. It's a breathtaking sight. As you stare transfixed, you instinctively reach for your wife's hand. At the same time, you gaze lovingly at your daughter to share this magic moment with her.

Debbi, however, is busily inspecting her skirt, smoothing out some imaginary wrinkles. As you watch, stupefied, she picks at her stockings, then lifts up her heels and turns her attention to the soles of her shoes.

Perhaps you fight the urge to ask her what in God's name is so important about her clothes when you took her to see King Tut who, for crying out loud, is lying there just a few inches in front of her nose. Or perhaps you're the type who says nothing at all, but simply s-t-a-r-e-s long and hard, seething inside that your daughter could be so disrespectful after all you've done to bring her to this wonderful place.

These are understandable "me-oriented" reactions—but they are knee-jerk responses. They are not adolescent-driven actions; they do not follow from a true understanding of adolescent behavior patterns. They fail to take into account the underlying reason for her preoccupation with her appearance, and her seeming indifference to a wrapped-up Egyptian who's been dead for about thirty centuries. Debbi is thinking not, as you are, about King Tut and the wonders of the ancient world, but rather about dinner, and about Lance, a boy she has heard so much about (from you), yet has never met. She is worried she might not be wearing the right thing, or perhaps doesn't look good enough, or maybe her shoes don't match her outfit . . . .

Whatever her specific concerns, they arise from real adolescent needs: to appeal to a fellow adolescent of the opposite sex. Debbi did not set out to ruin your day, or show ingratitude, or make you feel like a buffoon for thinking she'd appreciate King Tut; she simply has more immediate, and to an adolescent, more important concerns on her mind. Perhaps if you hadn't invited your old roommate and his son to dinner, her reaction to King Tut would be different (and perhaps it would not). Your job as a POA is to distance yourself from the behavior and respond to its meaning, rather than to react to the behavior itself.

You're driving with a business partner, trying to explain a sophisticated marketing strategy, and your son, sitting in the back seat, spends the entire ride interrupting with irrelevant questions, inane observations, and smart aleck comments. You need to see that his behavior is not rude, disrespectful, or embarrassing to *you*, but rather that it is an expression of your son's powerlessness. He is attempting to establish himself as a participant in your adult world. Or perhaps he is feeling lonely and this is his way of trying to elicit a response from a father who seems always to have time for his business associates, but never for his son.

Whatever the reason for your adolescent's actions, the key is to recognize that, while the behavior may appear to be directed at you as the target, in reality there is a perfectly logical, if unstated and perhaps unconscious meaning behind that action.

Or take the all-too-common pierced ear controversy (we're talking about boys' ears, of course). As a POA, you can knee-jerk react to an earring from your own point of view—no son of mine is going to walk around looking like a daughter of mine—or you can draw a deep breath, take a giant step back, and view pierced ears as a generational symbol, or even a fad, not too different really from Nehru jackets or Davy Crockett caps. Admittedly, those are not easy breaths or steps to take, but they are imperative if you and your children are to survive adolescence.

Having said all that we have said about adolescence, we must now note that there are indeed times when it is best for you simply to say or do nothing at all.

When your 13-year-old son says, "Dad, how come you drive me to church every Sunday, but you go off and play golf?"; when your 15-year-old daughter asks, "Mom, was your sex life better before you got married?"; when your 16-year-old son inquires, "How much pot did you smoke in college?"—these are situations when you must take more than a deep breath. At those moments, you have to realize that simply because you are a POA, you need not feel forced to answer every question the instant it is asked—or ever. You must be willing to say, "That's a good question, dear, but I'm not ready to answer it right now. I need time to think"—or even, "That's a subject I don't think is appropriate to discuss with you." Later in this book, we'll consider how and when to *not* answer your adolescent's questions.

We've raised a number of different issues of concern to all POAs in this chapter, including "testing the limits" behavior, fads and friends, and separation and independence; we haven't even mentioned such other crucial concepts as parental expectations of scholastic success, substance use, sexuality, and motivational problems. But all the ideas we've touched upon share a common thread: They're issues regarding values. And before you can understand your adolescent's values, you must first understand your own.

2 | Your Values, Your Adolescent

"Values" is an intimidating word for many of us. When we hear the term, we think of moral imperatives such as the Ten Commandments—long lists of "thou shalt not's," etched in stone. We shirk from thinking about values because if we admit that we have them, we may also have to admit that we don't always live up to them.

But values are not carved in stone. Remember, Moses himself smashed the first commandments in a fit of rage. Rather, values are standards, guideposts, ideals—concepts, not federal statutes—that can help us cope with the exigencies of daily life. Values are guidelines by which we would like to live our lives, although sometimes we fail to follow them.

Most of us, for example, would say that we believe in the value "Never tell a lie." But we also know that from time to time, we do fudge the truth. The telephone rings, and we tell our daughter, "Ask who it is. If it's Mrs. Baker, tell her I'm not in." Or we leave early on vacation and rather than risk the ire of the school attendance dean, we write a note excusing our son's absence "due to illness." Or we bring supplies from the office and use them at home, or tell our 13-year-old in the movie theater line, "It's okay, just say you're 12."

Are these actual lies or are they minor evasions that ease our daily routines? Does the way in which we answer the phone, write notes, use supplies, or buy tickets mean that we have abandoned certain values we say we cherish? These questions, which philosophers have devoted entire lives to studying, lie outside the realm of this book. But they do raise an important point. Before you can learn to be an effective POA and gain the courage to say no, before you can deal effectively with your adolescent, you must first take time to reflect on your own value system.

Unfortunately, you are placed in a difficult spot, because no matter how much examining you do, you cannot know all your values, and no matter how committed you are to trying, you cannot uphold every value at all times. It is just not possible. And worse, all adolescents have a built-in mechanism that finds every lapse and hypocrisy and hones right in on them. This is an irresistible challenge to them, and one they accept gladly.

However, to the extent that you do not examine your values and how you live by them, you are creating the field upon which endless power struggles will be played and lost. There will be no winners, only losers: parents and adolescents alike. Power struggles are not fun; they are painful and counterproductive, both to your sense of responsible parenting and self-esteem, and to your adolescent's growing sense of responsibility and self-esteem.

Another conundrum for parents of teenagers is that there remain some unresolved issues from your own adolescence that you are living with—and they will tend to be the same ones (or similar enough ones to those your adolescent is struggling with) to cause high anxiety, doubts, and fears.

Some of your values may conflict with other values that you have, and some of your behavior may clash with the values you hold most dear. Being called to task about such inconsistencies—being confronted with and criticized for your own behavior by your own adolescent—is one of the most difficult aspects of parenting. But if you are aware of your internal struggle before the inevitable confrontation, you will be well ahead of the game. You will be prepared to respond creatively and nondefensively.

If, however, you are caught unaware of those conflicts within yourself, you'll soon know it. Your responses will be defensive, rigid, authoritarian, or retaliatory. You'll know it because you will feel a combination of rage, helplessness, and guilt; you'll want to strike out or give up. It is a difficult task to have to deal with not only your child's adolescence but your own lingering adolescent problems at the same time. Perhaps you hoped that you left all that behind when your teenage years ended, and you resent being forced to relive the all-too-familiar discomforts of examining your own values and setting limits to your own behavior.

You must understand that values cannot be demanded, dictated, or enforced; they can only be demonstrated, emphasized, and lived. Once you realize that values are simply ideals, rather than laws, then it becomes easier to understand both your own adherence (and nonadherence) to values, and your adolescent's struggle to create his own value system.

And you'll also take a giant stride toward acknowledging adolescence not as an interminable power struggle but as an exciting opportunity to help your adolescent use her developing values to gain power over her own life.

THE TRANSMISSION OF VALUES IN DIFFERENT WAYS

It's your birthday, and in celebration your family has taken you to dinner at your favorite restaurant. The waiter was attentive, the food delicious, and your children engaged in only a minimal amount of pesky behavior. As they proudly pool their money—it's their treat, after all—you rise from the table, filled with the warm glow of fatherhood. Pulling the car keys from your pocket, you head for the exit.

"Wait, Dad, you're not going to drive, are you?" Brad, your youngest, asks, his awkward thirteen-year-old voice filled with concern.

"What? Of course I'm going to drive. How do you think we got here?" you respond, a bit puzzled. What's he getting at? Wait a minute, you think. They wouldn't be surprising you with a new car, would they . . . .

"Dad, you can't drive. You just had wine!" Brad says, genuinely alarmed (and a bit too loud, for your taste). The couple at the next table look up, interested. Visions of a new Jeep vanish as quickly as they came.

"Brad, I had *one glass* of wine. I hardly think I'm unfit to drive—and I don't think you should be the judge of that, either." You stride emphatically toward the door, signifying an end to the discussion.

But Brad, nearly running to catch up to you and making a minor scene in the process, isn't ready to surrender. "C'mon, Dad," he pleads. "We just went over this stuff in health on Friday. One glass of wine is the same as a shot of whiskey. It takes about an hour to get absorbed in your bloodstream. You didn't even finish it until Mom had coffee. Dad, you're not supposed to drink and drive! We saw a movie on it, and Coach B said it." He pauses now for dramatic effect, a regular Laurence Olivier of the temperance movement. "And you always say it, too!"

You walk out into the parking lot, swinging your keys around your index finger to show that you're in control—of the keys, your faculties, and this argument that should never have occurred. You're a prudent, law-abiding adult who has had one glass of wine with dinner; you've been drinking for over twenty-five years, and have never had so much as a fender-bender. Your son is 13, has taken one health course, and probably can't even tell the difference between white wine and lite beer.

Out of the corner of your eye, you see him look up at your wife. Urgently, he pleads: "Mom!" You reach for the door; if you can get in quickly, close it and start the engine, this idiotic discussion will be over.

, But your wife is there first. Quietly, she says, "Honey, if Brad can't get *you* to not drink and drive, how can he ever get his friends to?"

Immediately, you see her point. She's right; your value system does say, "Don't drink and drive." Some complex concepts are involved here—the difference between social drinking and heavy drinking; a son taking issue with his father in public; your desire to show respect for what your child learns in school. But these concepts only obscure the more important issue: upholding your value about drinking and driving.

You hand your wife the keys and slide into the passenger seat.

You've just given a wonderful lesson to your son. You've affirmed your value system—and supported your son in his search to define his own. You've shown respect for your son's judgment, and for your wife's. And you've done it despite your own misgivings about what he was up to. Your son was quick to test—even assault—the limits of your value system and in this case you took a step back, examined those values, and found that the best course of action was simply to affirm them.

Upon reflection you realized that in the years before he became an adolescent, your son was constantly exposed to the values by which you live your life. Out of a desire to please you, he adopted some by copying your behavior. Now, in adolescence, as he strives to develop his own value system, he is testing and challenging some of those ideals he once mimicked. He has chewed on your value system for many years; now it is time for him to decide whether to swallow it whole, spit it out, or try to digest those parts that are most palatable to him.

Rose came from a family that always valued education. Her mother was a teacher, as was her grandmother. Her father never doubted that she would earn at least one degree—but she did him one better, and after majoring in math in college got her M.B.A. when her children were still young. Now she's been a bank vice president for five years. Her husband has a graduate degree in journalism and works in publishing.

Rose's son Scott, 19, was a sophomore at an Ivy League university, heading for med school. He was a musician, and an honor student all the way. Her daughter Robin, 16, received A's and B's as a high school freshman. She showed less interest in grades her sophomore year, and as a junior—when grades "really count"—she began working even less. But she had a beautiful voice, sang with a high school music group, played guitar, and was active in the school drama organization.

Robin began to tell her parents things like, "You know, you really don't need a college degree to succeed in life. It used to make a difference, but not any more. Anyway, I'm really interested in being a vocalist; I want to make records and videos. And, I mean, a college degree just isn't going to help. It would just be a four year waste of my time and your money."

Her parents were, naturally, horrified—not that she wanted to become the next Madonna but that she suddenly seemed to have devalued the family's commitment to formal education.

"I'll go through the motions if you make me," Robin said. "I'll take SATs, apply to college, but I may decide not to go. Or I may drop out. I'll just have to find out on my own the best way to become a star."

Her parents wondered what had gone wrong. Had Scott stolen the spotlight? Had his extraordinary academic achievement dulled Robin's drive toward her own level of excellence? Could they live with a child who might end up as "only" a high school graduate? Where had they failed? They took Robin's change of direction as a personal blow—their own failure.

They called Scott at college: Did he know anything about this? Sure, he said; she'd been talking about wanting to be a performer for a couple of years. Hadn't they noticed how much time she spent rehearsing with her group? All of them want to be entertainers, he added. They asked about the academic goals of the others in the group. Of the six, Scott said, only two were planning to go to college.

Perplexed as to how they could have missed understanding the impact of the group's influence on their daughter, they called the school guidance counselor. He said he was unaware that Robin was considering not going to college.

In addition to valuing education, Robin's parents had always said they valued "following your star"—except they wanted that path to pass through a four-year college course of study. How could they help Robin follow *that* route? they wondered. Giving orders to their children was not the way they had parented in the past. Although they were sorely tempted to tell her she would be "cut off" from funds if she did not go to college—and, worse, perhaps cut off from their emotional support as well—they stuck to their belief that "pulling rank" was not a productive way of teaching their children how to make intelligent decisions for themselves.

They also resisted the "How could you do this to our family?" guilt trip. They *were* prepared, however, to try to redirect her thinking toward the benefit of a college education in the music business. Giving credence to the value that decisions should be made not on impulse but only after reflection and study, they made contacts in the music industry, gathered data and began to introduce Robin to people who could tell her about the music world. They and their contacts hoped Robin would see a more realistic musical picture. Robin was willing to talk to the people her parents found because they presented it as information upon which she could make a better decision—and because Robin's parents kept quiet after making the initial introductions.

They also worked with Robin's guidance counselor to find several colleges with good performing arts departments. But most importantly, they refused to enter into a power struggle with Robin, or to "pull rank" on her. Those methods did not appeal to them; they preferred to gather data for her and to explore options with her.

Eventually, Robin did go to college—for two years. Then she took a year off, trying to gain a foothold in the music industry. Ultimately she settled for a summer internship in a recording studio, and then returned to school to earn a bachelor of fine arts degree.

No one's values had been compromised—neither the adolescent's nor her parents'. Robin felt she was making decisions for herself along the way, and her parents felt they were playing the role of supportive, encouraging adults. And they all were correct.

Throughout this book, we will attempt to show how you, as a POA, can take a potentially explosive situation such as the one we've just discussed, and turn it into positive, "value-able" lessons. However, unlike the drinking and driving incident, many times you will have to say no to your adolescent.

How do you do it?

One way is by first assessing your own values. You must confront your own ideals from a nondefensive point of view and then, through a process of examination and refinement, develop a sense of when, where, and how it is appropriate to say no to your adolescent. You will never be able to successfully survive your son's or daughter's adolescence unless you first feel comfortable with your own values.

One of the real problems of being a POA is that as an adult your values are formed, and you live your life without questioning them. Just as you do not think consciously about how you brush your teeth, you also do not dwell consciously on the ideals that govern your life. However, adolescent's question their values and your values every day. The incessant barrage of questions—"Why *can't* I stay out until midnight on weekends?" "What does it *matter* if I don't comb my hair?" "How come *you* always volunteer to chaperone the dances?"—you are forced to scrutinize those values constantly.

Without realizing it, teenagers make you dig deep, to search for answers that are not readily available. You're not used to doing that and find the process of self-examination annoying, tiring, perhaps even painful. That's one of the reasons that although deep down you know adolescents are striving, as they should, to grow into mature adults, you nevertheless get impatient or angry with them. It is no fun having your authority and values tested twenty-five hours a day, eight days a week.

However, you will never be comfortable with your values today unless you look back a few decades to your own adolescence. (And we urge you to take that retrospective kindly. Examine with compassion your own teenage years, so that you may gaze more empathically on your adolescent's current journey.) When you were an adolescent, you probably made a fashion statement at some point—with clothes, hair or jewelry—that upset your parents. Now, your adolescent is doing the same thing.

Your daughter Kara has taken to wearing black—all black, all the time. Her entire wardrobe—shirts, pants, belts, shoes, socks, even hair feathers—is black. Her friends, boys as well as girls, dress similarly, and for the life of you, you can't figure out why a group of good-looking kids would want to spend their teenage years looking like a permanent funeral procession.

You have no idea how she acquired this depressing collection of clothes. Wearing black makes some kind of political statement you don't understand, but you know you don't like it. To you, looking neat, clean, and attractive is important—and all black just doesn't do it. The color smacks of rebellion, bad taste, and thumbing one's nose at all the values you hold about good grooming.

Over the years you've invested plenty of time and energy in looking well put together—and in Kara's looking the same. For as long as you can remember, she has been your shopping companion; until several months ago she valued your opinion and admired your taste in just about everything. Only last summer, before her twelfth birthday, you had a wonderful time hitting all the local shops. You bought her a beautiful (and very with-it) wardrobe; it stretched your budget, but you wanted to buy her everything she said would make her an "in" seventh grader.

She was thrilled, excited, even grateful. Now not only does she not wear any of those things but she won't even listen to your views on the subject of clothes. And she flat out refuses to shop with you anymore. You feel a loss; you're hurt and disappointed. And when you shift into your more logical mode, you are puzzled and more than a little concerned.

The look galls you enough most of the time, and your stomach knots up every morning when she walks into your sun-filled kitchen, draped from head to toe in gloomy black, but a bigger problem looms. Your niece's confirmation is coming up, and Kara has announced that she'll be wearing her favorite color scheme to church or she won't be going at all. You're worrying more and more each day about what the rest of the congregation will think and say when Kara shows up for this joyous occasion doing her best imitation of the world's youngest widow.

You can't tell her not to go to the confirmation; it is a family occasion and, besides, Kara likes her cousin. Bringing up the color issue one more time causes your heart to pound. She gets so antagonistic and defensive when the topic is school clothes, you can just imagine what sparks will fly when the church gets dragged into this. Kara seems to have seized control of the situation, and you're the one who is suffering doubt, anxiety, and stomach pains because of it.

At this point, you must look beyond the immediate issue of black clothes, and examine your own value system. You must question your own reasons for worry, and balance your concern over what your friends and family will think about your daughter's attire against her own need to be independent, to test the limits of conventionality.

Sure she's experimenting, taking risks, by flouting the accepted standards of society (at least as they apply to church confirmations). But who is she hurting? Is your embarrassment more important than her assertion of independence? And since she does not lock herself away in her room, listening to heavy metal bands while writing desperate poetry, you know her black phase is not indicative of suicidal thoughts.

On the other hand, if you do allow her to wear black to her cousin's confirmation, will she take this as a signal that she can test other limits, such as curfew or drinking? Would the reception be best served by a happy, black-clad daughter, a sullen, colorfully garbed one—or none at all?

As you ask yourself these questions, it might be helpful to think back to the days when you were 14. How did you dress and look? Did your friends dress and look the same? Was it ever an issue with parents, teachers or other adults?

If you examine your own past and current values honestly, you may come to the conclusion that wearing black is not an antisocial statement, or a sly means of embarrassing one's family in church, but a normal way for an adolescent to act. You may recall long-ago arguments over the band jacket you wore everywhere, even to church, and recognize that wearing black and wearing a band jacket are not dissimilar. They are, rather, the means by which an adolescent identifies and associates with a peer group that has like-minded interests, and the way an adolescent separates from her parents and establishes a sense of self.

You may not particularly like the look by which she chooses to assert her independence, but your opinion is not the issue. Wearing black is within the normal range of adolescent behavior, and that's what counts.

By this point, it must be clear that when we talk about "having the courage to say no" to your adolescent, we are not simply dishing up a warmed-over version of the "tough love" approach to parenting that was briefly popular back in the '80s.

Having the courage to say no is not nearly as easy as that. It is much more complex than laying down a few hard and fast rules—some do's and don'ts, a few can's and can'ts. It goes beyond delivering ultimatums or planting "do not cross" signs in the front yard of family relationships, then bolting the door the instant your adolescent challenges just one of them.

Those are black and white reactions, not applicable to adolescence, which is filled with more shades of gray than a paint store.

"Tough love" may work in certain drastic situations—physical abuse, repeated law-breaking, heroin addiction

—but the vast majority of adolescent and family problems are not drastic. They are often aggravating, sometimes serious, yet seldom life-threatening. They are normal responses to the hormonal and societal demands of adolescence, and although the range of adolescents' behavior patterns can seem bewildering, rest assured that much of it is indeed normal.

So forget "tough love." Forget screaming "You will do this, that, and the other thing—or else!" every half hour. Forget barring the gate if your demands are disobeyed. That kind of response to your adolescent's actions takes plenty of physical strength and energy, but not much creativity. And being the parent of an adolescent demands industrial-size quantities of imagination and creativity. Consider this scene:

You, Max, are sitting with your wife, Carol Anne, son Robbie, 15, and daughter Missy, 13, at the dinner table. This is a rare occurrence, since your executive level position with an importing company takes you to the Far East at least one week each month (and re-entry requires several additional days of adjustment). In addition, you take plenty of domestic trips, overseeing offices up and down the West Coast.

Carol Anne has a good teaching position in town. Although she would lose her pension if the family moved to either coast, the decision to stay in the Midwest has been made primarily for the children's benefit. They are both doing well in school, have many friends and outside interests, and seem to have adjusted well to your frequent and lengthy absences. They are adamant about not upsetting the Midwestern apple cart, even though living further west would make better business and strategic sense to you.

An unspoken deal has been struck: You and your wife will not force a move on the children, in exchange for their continued exemplary behavior at home and in school. Unspoken agreements are common and to be expected among families, yet we are always rather surprised when they are articulated. Sometimes they are spoken in behavior rather than words, as this family drama unfolds.

Unbeknownst to you and your wife, Robbie has begun having some difficulties with the boys who have been his friends since fourth grade. Because the family balance depended on everyone's stability, Robbie was unable to tell his parents that he was feeling more and more isolated from his friends, and angry about the position he was in. He was beginning to feel worn down by his need to resist all the limit-stretching his friends felt entitled to (by their parents), and the need to behave so well in his own home (part of the unspoken deal he had made with you and Carol Anne).

Robbie was caught in a conflict between a desire to join the group and test his own limits, and his fear of breaking the unspoken deal with his parents, which he knew could propel the family to the West Coast on very short notice. He could not risk getting into any kind of trouble, yet he wanted to stay with a group from which he was becoming more and more alienated. He was afraid, too, his sister would never forgive him if he "caused" the family to move, and he worried about his mother, for whom he had assumed a care-taking role in his father's absence. Talk about a double—or triple—bind! Robbie was bursting to try something.

With that bit of background, let's return to the seemingly picture perfect dinner table, where the conversation is proceeding pleasantly enough. Around the middle of the main course, Robbie asks for something. However, instead of asking you for the vegetables, he says, "Max, could you please pass the peas?"

He says this calmly, politely—in fact, so casually you almost missed it. But there's no mistaking what he said. Your son addressed you by your first name.

You've already started to reach for the peas when it hits you, and you realize, simultaneously, that you don't have a clue how to respond. Swiftly, you opt for the path of least resistance—passing the peas, pretending you didn't hear, hoping it was a once-in-a-lifetime choice of phrasing—when Missy stokes the fire.

"Hey, how come Robbie gets to call you Max? How old do I have to be before I can say Max too?"

Instantly, in the time it takes to pass peas from one side of the table to the other, you've got to examine all your beliefs about the equality of parent-child relationships (a corner of your value system you never before realized existed), while at the same time formulating a clear, concise response.

Should you shrug off the incident as you'd swat away a fly—"Whenever you feel old enough, hon"—or should you draw a sharper distinction between a 15-year-old boy and his 13-year-old sister? Then a third, more disturbing question pops into your head: Is this an Issue, a hill worth dying on? And if it is, what's the proper method of attack?

Sitting there, a bowlful of peas in your hand, you've got to deal with a host of questions. Is Robbie being disrespectful? Playful? Challenging? Teasing? Is he experimenting, and if so, is 15 the right age to do it? Is he telling you subconsciously that he views the two of you as equals, and now wishes to be treated that way? Or is he merely aping the actions of a friend he admires?

Because you are caught off guard, you don't even think that Robbie's out-of-character behavior is merely a message to you that something is not right with him. Furthermore,

Missy's jumping on the bandwagon keeps the issue focused along the "values offended" line, which clearly is the case for you. Your wife is looking relieved that she does not have to handle this one, since in your family direct communication is handled directly, without interference by the other parent.

Your job is to examine (in the span of a few seconds) your own values, and determine how you feel about Robbie's comment (and Missy's lightning-quick follow-up). Do you feel threatened? Hurt? Guilty? Embarrassed? Mad? And—most important—why?

How you answer those questions will determine your response. There is no "right answer" here; right answers are for the SATs. In fact, your response might range from a cool, casual "You can call me anything. Just don't call me late for dinner" to a more thought-provoking "That's a good question, Missy. What do you think, Rob?" The phrasing or content of the response is less important than the fact that it be your own answer, phrased your unique way, developed from an honest analysis of your own value system—values you hope to impart to your value-seeking adolescents.

Such a response sets a tone, a nonconfrontational, yet value-affirming, tone. That tone should send the message that you're the parent, they're the kids, and in your family limits are going to be set. They're not going to be set arbitrarily, dictatorially, or thunderously, but they will be set.

And in setting limits, with justice, empathy and a sense of humor, you affirm your own value system. You establish a structure, boundaries, limits, whatever you want to call them, through which family living is made enjoyable (or, for the moment, at least bearable). You send the message that, while you realize it is often appropriate for adolescents to take risks, to verbalize new ideas and explore previously forbidden territories, you also know that certain impulsive words and deeds can lead to disaster.

That's where having the courage to say no differs from "tough love."

Your adolescent is, as we're sure you've noticed, testing you and your values in ways that have never been tested before. The charming little tyke who a short while ago adored being dressed, dangled, and driven around by you now finds fault with the minutest details of your life: the way you speak, look, shop, answer the phone, salt your food, back out of the driveway. You—the omniscient parent who, for more than a decade, has been in the pleasant, ego-reinforcing business of dispensing advice—suddenly find yourself on the far less enjoyable receiving end. And most of that advice is delivered in anything but a helpful or constructive tone of voice.

Your two first natural reactions of defending yourself or out-yelling your adolescent just won't work. Either one might make you feel better, or temporarily reaffirm your position as "master" or "mistress" of your battle-weary household, but neither reaction will help you tread the fine line between squelching your adolescent's impulsive, risk-taking experimentation, and assisting him in his natural drive toward independence and autonomy. And ultimately, of course, your job as the parent of an adolescent is to take life- and family-destroying negative impulses and turn them into positive, life- and family-affirming ones.

WHEN VALUES DIFFER

Much of what we've said in this chapter has been directed at parents—the assumption being that Mother and Father function as a well-oiled piston, synchronous and complementary on all issues relating to the upbringing of their child. But in reality, we know, such teamwork isn't always possible.

What happens when one partner places a high priority on mealtime togetherness, while the other prefers informal eating on the run? What happens when a child wants to date at 13, which one parent thinks is wonderfully exciting, and the other deems completely inappropriate? Or when spouses disagree about an 18-year-old's desire to vacation with friends, rather than with the rest of the family?

If parents are in conflict about a particular value—perhaps we should say "when," not "if," for such disagreements are inevitable—it is imperative that they recognize what is happening and find a way to compromise. Otherwise, open and visible contradictions will undermine everything else you both say and do, and then none of your values will be viewed as meaningful or worthy of emulation.

When parents disagree, they should retire to a back room, discuss their positions and emerge with a reasonable consensus, which they then present to their child as the view they both hold. Disagreements are a normal, even healthy, part of a marriage, but they should not intrude on the all-important job of value-directing that you and your coparent must share.

VALUES IN THE NONTRADITIONAL FAMILY

The various types of nontraditional families are many: single-parent families; blended families; families in which one parent lives with, but is not married to, a "significant other"; families with gay parents. Such family constellations are growing in number, as are the numbers of children and adults living in them.

The concepts we present in this book are valid and important in any family situation, and not just those with two married, biological parents. The job of parenting is the same, whatever the description of the parent. But if you find your-self in a situation without a coparent to back you up (and this may also occur, we should note, in "traditional" two-parent families), you may find it significantly more difficult to hold fast to your family values.

In such circumstances, you must make a special effort to be consistent. The live-in boyfriend must back up the mother's values and decisions just as consistently as if he were the father of her children; the divorced parents who can barely look at each other without initiating combat must set aside their personal enmity when parenting issues arise; the widowed father struggling to raise his child, with the help of his mother, must make certain that her "parenting" is as consistent as his own wife's would have been; the partner of a gay parent must be as strong and supportive as the part-ner of a nongay parent.

For this to occur, there must be honest and constant communication between all adults involved—whether they coexist in the same house, share custody of a child on a semiweekly basis, or live thousands of miles apart. In order for a stepparent to overcome the daunting "But you're not my father!" challenge, he must first spend time talking about the fact that he is not her father with his stepdaughter's mother. To avoid the strife that results when separated parents spout wildly contrasting values and expectations whenever their children are in their clutches, two people who no longer have anything else in common must verbal-ize their ideas, for the good of the children they still share. This should be done privately, of course; the last thing adolescents need to hear is a reprise of the same old "Don't you realize the problems you're causing your father and me?" song.

In certain families—intact as well as divorced, blended, merged or whatever—open dialogue is, unfortunately, impossible; in others, the situation is so stressful, because of death or abandonment, that the sole remaining parent feels overwhelmed by his or her responsibility. In such cases, we advise seeking professional help.

Talking to a therapist or counselor is not a sign of weakness; it is an indication of strength. There come times in all our lives when we need the help of a neutral third party to help us sort out the issues that overwhelm us. Men and women trained professionally in family dynamics but who stand outside the family circle can render invaluable services in times of stress. It is the intelligent, healthy parent who recognizes their worth.

ACHIEVING POSITIVE VALUES FROM SAYING NO

You may have noticed in this chapter that although we discussed saying no, our three vignettes did not end with "no" responses. Although this book is indeed entitled *You Can Say No to Your Teenager*, it is important to understand that saying no is not a thoughtless, autocratic, negative response to any type of threatening, aberrant, or odd behavior.

Saying no stems instead from a position of strength and security. Parents of adolescents who can say no have already looked back on their own adolescence; have already confronted and analyzed their own value systems from a nondefensive position (and continue that process), and are thus able to say no to their adolescents comfortably and quietly, at appropriate times and over appropriate issues. In so doing, they strengthen and affirm not only their adolescents' own value systems but those of the entire family as well. Any parent who has the courage to say no has learned how to turn an adolescent's negative behavior patterns into positive actions, which in turn buoys the experience of the entire family.

And the parent does this by understanding that just as adolescence is a *process* of growing into adulthood, so too is being the parent of an adolescent a process. It is a process of recognizing different types of behaviors and actions, of determining which are normal and which are not, and of learning how to channel normal impulses in a creative, purposeful direction.

Being able to say no, then, actually means having the courage to say yes: yes to the positive value system you have embraced and that you hope your family will embrace.

But how do you determine what is normal behavior, and what is not? How can you tell when experimentation crosses the line and becomes dangerous? How do you know when, where, and how to say no? The rest of the book will help provide answers to those questions and help you deal with the specific perils and pitfalls of adolescence.

3 The Meaning of Behavior

All behavior has meaning.

Of course, it's often difficult to cut through the smoke of the behavior battle and discover exactly what that meaning is. To illustrate, we'll begin with a few all-too-common examples.

You're driving your daughter Kyra, who has just had her fifteenth birthday, to the annual "Snowball Fling" dance. She has been talking about the dance all week and has mentioned often that most of the girls will be going by themselves—not "with dates." She has not indicated any reluctance at having you drive her to the dance, making a point of asking that you be sure to get her there on time.

Appropriately, it's snowing; she is dressed fashionably, which is to say minimally according to your standards. She prefers not to be burdened with such impediments as coat, scarf, and gloves. As you approach the school, the radio blares an unintelligible tune, and Kyra seems happy and anticipatory. Thus you're perplexed and more than a little upset when Kyra announces rather imperially, "Dad, you don't have to drive all the way in. Just let me out here; I'll walk the rest of the way myself."

You are accompanying your son, a high school senior, to his first college interview, eager to give him some of the wonderful moral support you've been storing away for just such a stressful situation. He's been quiet throughout the long drive, even when the queries concern relatively neutral subjects such as the weather, the traffic, and why people wear neckties. You attribute his silence to nerves, and wait patiently for the opening to deliver your pep talk. Suddenly, on the steps of the admissions office and with no advance warning, he turns to you and lashes out: "Mom, I'm perfectly capable of doing this myself! I don't know why you have to tag along everywhere I go. Why don't you just sit in the car and wait 'til I'm through, huh?"

You've looked forward for years to the day your daughter can join you in sharing environmental concerns. As a family, you have been involved in ecological education projects, talking often about aerosol cans, the ozone layer, and the disappearance of rain forests. You've stressed recycling efforts, the purchase and use of biodegradable products, and the avoidance of insecticides and weed killers. Yet your daughter seems to go willfully out of her way to *not* stack newspapers, stuffing them instead into whatever waste-basket is handy. Not only will she *not* boycott products you've identified as being environmentally unacceptable, she goes out of her way to purchase such items whenever she has the opportunity. She won't even keep her bottles and cans in the box you've set by the door, although you've gone so far as to volunteer to return the collected containers to the store.

All of these examples are simply variations on a theme; we could have chosen dozens of other vignettes, but you get the idea. Your teenager is acting in a manner that either implicitly or explicitly seems to reject not only you but all you've ever done and stood for. After years spent preparing your child to handle any social, emotional, or intellectual challenge thrown his or her way, the first time you are asked—no, told—to butt out can be devastating.

But remember that all behavior has meaning, even behavior that seems as obstinate and immature as that depicted in our three examples. And before you, as a POA, can understand the meaning of such behavior, you must first take that crucial step backward: Take a deep breath and avoid that oh-so-tempting knee-jerk response. Rather than reacting in the passion of the moment, try to take a dis-passionate view of your child's behavior; view it nonjudg-mentally, even empathetically.

What you will see by stepping aside and not involving yourself via an equally sharp response (as your teenager hopes you will) is that your adolescent's behavior is *not* a statement of dislike for you as a parent, nor is it a personal rejection of you as a human being. It is, rather, a demonstration of her need to independently assert her separation from you. Your adolescent is engaged in a perfectly natural, completely desirable—even entirely necessary—search for her own personality, and in that search, it becomes necessary for her to understand that she is different from her parents. She needs to know that, far from being a clone of Mom and Dad, she is in fact someone quite separate from them.

Thus you should see your adolescent's apparent rejection of you not as a painful smack to your pride but rather as a positive affirmation that so far you've done a good job of raising your child. You've brought your adolescent to the brink of independence, and now, by behaving in a manner that says "I want to walk into the dance myself"; "I need to test myself in this stressful college admissions situation without any outside help"; "I'm not my parent. My mom is concerned with ecology, so I won't be," your teenager is acting precisely as he or she should at this point in adolescence.

STEPPING BACK AND EXAMINING THE BEHAVIOR

Now that you understand the need to step back and gaze nonjudgmentally at your adolescent's behavior patterns, it is important to reintroduce the notion of values in order to better understand the meaning of the behavior.

You are a well-known real estate agent working in the community in which you live; your husband is a high school principal in a neighboring town. You have structured your job so as to be available at least some of the afternoons when your children (Jack, 18; Melinda, 16; and Marc, 11) return home from school. Although you cannot be there every day, you certainly feel you are not an absentee parent.

All three children seem to be moving ahead with their lives in relatively comfortable fashion. Jack is a freshman at the college he always wanted to attend, pursuing his career goal in computers and engineering at the campus radio station. Melinda, a high school junior, has a B average, is heavily involved in drama, and works part-time as a cashier at a local supermarket. Marc, a sixth grader, is achieving well although he is somewhat learning disabled. He has come to terms with the slight interferences his disability creates (and with some of the mechanisms he has had to develop to compensate).

Melinda has landed a key role in the fall production of *Guys and Dolls* and has adjusted her work schedule to meet the demands of play practice. One afternoon, as you are organizing the next day's laundry, you receive a call from the teacher directing the show.

"Mrs. Marshall, this is Margaret Erickson. I'm calling to see if Melinda is ill. She didn't appear for rehearsal today, and since she's usually one of the kids I know I can count on, I thought I'd check with you. None of the others knew where she was."

You are momentarily taken aback, since Melinda had left for school at the usual time, and she did not call you at the office to say anything was wrong. You quickly organize your thoughts and decide to be up front and direct.

"Actually, Melinda was at school today, I believe. She left this morning, and I haven't heard anything since."

"I'm sorry to be the bearer of bad news, but I thought it was important to let you know. Like I said, Melinda is so dependable . . ."

"Thanks," you reply. "I'll take it up with her as soon as I see her."

When you hang up, you find yourself flooded with emotions. You are worried and angry, of course, but also confused. Where is Melinda? Why did she skip play practice? You review last evening's events to see if you can discover any triggering events for your daughter's somewhat out-of-character behavior.

Melinda returns home for dinner at the time she normally would be back from rehearsal.

"Hi, honey," you greet her. "Anything new with the play today?"

"No Mom, just the usual stuff. Ms. Erickson was really hyper today—she was on everybody's case. I mean, if you missed a cue she went berserk."

Now you're in a quandary. Your daughter has skipped play practice, and now is lying about it. Should you confront her directly? Do you attempt to trap her into admitting the truth? Or do you not say anything at all, hoping it is just an aberration?

Keeping in mind the contents of this chapter, you might decide to say something like, "Melinda, we both know you weren't at rehearsal today, so we're not going to argue about whether you were there or not. Let's see if we can try to find out why you skipped, and hope to help you avoid this kind of thing in the future."

In fact, Melinda's behavior may be an attempt to declare that even very responsible people sometimes can behave in less than responsible ways. A variation of this is also possible: She may wonder what the consequences will be if she gives in to this impulsive wish, even though she knows it is wrong. Or she may be wondering whether anyone will take note of "Miss Responsibility," or whether they will simply try to ignore her unusual behavior.

There are other possibilities. Maybe Melinda is trying to assert that *she* will decide for herself what constitutes responsible behavior, rather than simply accepting adult rules. Or maybe she is saying something on the order of "I don't know how to behave when I think it's stupid to follow orders. I already know my lines; it's the other people who haven't done their work."

By stepping back and examining behavior you could emerge with an understanding of any of the situations suggested above. Clearly, you have not attacked or belittled your daughter but rather opened the dialogue and invited her participation.

Although you're a successful businessman and esteemed civic leader, you have not forgotten the allure sports held for you as a youth. You are not only an adult fan but also a participant (racquetball, softball, volleyball). You were a pretty good high school athlete (if you do say so yourself), but of all your sports you loved football the best. You reveled in your understanding of strategy, and the thrill of the contact of blocking and tackling. When your son Matthew was born you were delighted, as you thought ahead to the years of football togetherness ahead. The animals on his first pajamas were (Miami) Dolphins and (Philadelphia) Eagles, not little lambs and ducks, and for as far back as you can remember, you and he have spent Saturdays and Sundays out in the backyard, chuckin' around the ol' pigskin.

Matthew played in the youth football league as soon as he weighed enough, and although he was never a star, you always admired the way he kept plugging away. He worked hard, practiced each assignment repeatedly and intensely, and attended each locker room chalk talk with enthusiasm. Being big and strong, he was never cut from the team.

Meanwhile, you put your time in too, as a coach and advisor to the football program. Now that Matthew is 14 you've been elected president of the town's Pop Warner League. The job takes a lot of time, cutting into hours you could spend with your family. There are meetings to run, coaches to recruit and check up on, fields and equipment to oversee, schedules to organize and rules to enforce—but it's worth it. You are heavily involved in the sport you love, you provide an important service to your son and his teammates, and you are a well-known, respected member of the community.

The day before 14-year-old tryouts for the oldest, most prestigious team in the league, Matthew suddenly announces he will not be playing football this year. He delivers this pronouncement simply, with no embellishment; he offers little opportunity for discussion. The decision has been made, by Matthew.

Shocked, you search for some way to change his mind, but he is adamant. His closing words reverberate in your ears: "You can do whatever you want, but I'm not gonna play."

You are stunned, devastated, and embarrassed. You bombard yourself with questions: How can my son be a quitter? Why would he do this to me? What will the town think when the president of the entire league's kid doesn't even try out? What have I done wrong?

This is the perfect moment to take that step back and look at your values and at your own past, and to recognize how you got to be the person you are today. Examine the situation first not from Matthew's point of view, but rather from your own. Try to determine how you feel and to understand your own behavior as a first step toward understanding your son's feelings and behavior. As you follow this sequence, you can move toward figuring out what meaning underlies Matthew's behavior.

Your examination of your values might focus on the reasons you became so involved in Pop Warner in the first place. What were you acting upon in advancing from coach to president of the league? Did you do it because of Matthew's love for football—or your own? Were you attracted by the chance to become a big man in town, or to show your neighbors what a good father you are? Was it a representation of substitute achievement at organizational management you were not able to get at your job? Or did it perhaps represent a chance to get out of the house for a few hours each week?

Once you have honestly assessed your own values, motives, and behavior, then you might view your son's actions in a different light. Perhaps you'll be able to communicate with him by saying something like "Matthew, I've been thinking a lot about this. I was wondering if part of the problem is how much time I spent on football, and not at home . . . ."

There may not be any heart-to-heart dialogue after you say those words; your son may find it impossible to verbalize his feelings. Adolescents are often embarrassed when their parents are forthcoming. But Matthew's lack of response need not mean he hasn't heard what you are saying or understood what you mean. You should not measure the effectiveness of what you say or do by the presence (or absence) of some immediate response from your son. And even if you talk no more about it, your statement will mean something to him. Simply by stepping aside, avoiding a reflexive "Why me?" reaction, and studying your own values, you may come closer to understanding your son's seemingly hurtful behavior.

There are, of course, no pat answers to Matthew-style actions. Maybe you have put too much pressure on him; perhaps you have not, but still he feels unable to live up to your gridiron expectations of him. Possibly, your increasing involvement in football has taken away an activity he felt was "his"; perhaps he resents the time you spend with coaches and officials instead of with him; maybe he doesn't want to share you even with his teammates. Perhaps he just dislikes sports, and prefers music, writing, computers, or video games.

How do you find out whether your youngster is punishing you or, in a backhand way, "praising" you? In other words, how do you know which of the above interpretations is correct? Of course, there is no "correct" answer where adolescent behavior patterns are concerned; each child is unique and any one action might be the result of a complex combination of factors, only some of which may have been mentioned above.

The important thing is this: You know your child better than anyone and you know yourself. Learn to step back; avoid precipitous, judgmental responses; check your own values; then brainstorm for creative interpretations and explanations until you find one (or more) that fit your adolescent. You might liken this process to an archaeological dig in which you unearth many valuable and useful artifacts in the mysterious territory of adolescent behavior.

Let's look at another example:

For several months your daughter Meredith has worked hard learning to drive. She has taken driver's ed in school, pored over the less-than-riveting textbook at home, even survived your edgy advice during weekend sessions that have advanced from slow circles around the parking lot to ten miles an hour down side streets to a steady fifty-five on the interstate highway. You finally have as much confidence in her as any parent can have in an as-yet-unlicensed driver; you have accepted the fact that your little girl will soon round a big curve on the road toward independence, and you and your wife make plans for a small celebration the day Meredith actually receives that little laminated ticket to ride.

And then the Saturday night before her test, she takes your car without permission and clips a neighbor's mailbox, less than two blocks from home. She quietly enters your room to inform you of the incident, drops the car keys in your hand, and swiftly makes her way to her bedroom.

The knee-jerk response is easy. We'll delete the expletives, but you know the gist: "How could you be so careless? Why on earth weren't you paying attention? Do you realize what this will do to our insurance—which, young lady, you're not even covered for yet. And do you have any idea what could have happened to all of us if, God forbid, you hit a child instead of just a mailbox . . ."

But if you have learned that all behavior has meaning, you will understand that Meredith's two hundred–yard automotive adventure was not simply a wild, impulsive joyride. She might have been saying without using words that "A car is powerful; it's more freedom than I can handle.

I don't want the responsibility. Don't let me drive, even though I will loudly protest that I can."

This is a difficult situation, and not only because the livid, punitive response seems perfectly legitimate to you. Three sets of parents, all accurately reading the same "I feel scared about growing up" meaning into her behavior, might react in three dissimilar ways.

One set of parents might give structure to Meredith's worries by saying no—creatively—to her plan to take her test on Wednesday. They might set up a schedule under which she could earn back certain driving privileges, culminating in a new test date some number of months away. In discussions with her they might stress the need for responsible behavior, without actually accusing her of fearing new responsibilities. In this way, they can help her overcome her worries by showing her that she can, indeed, fulfill certain adult responsibilities.

Another set of parents might devise a different plan. They might agree to proceed with Meredith's test as scheduled, thus allowing her to save face with her peers—for getting one's license is a Very, Very Big Deal—while at the same time severely restrict her use of the car (once it's back from the shop). That way, Meredith will have her license, yet not have to face the responsibility of driving at times she does not want to. She will not feel overburdened by the awesome freedom the unlimited use of an automobile can bring.

Meanwhile, a third set of parents might decide upon taking a step back and examining their own values. Perhaps her message to them is: "A license will give me not only freedom but also the responsibility of chauffeuring my little brothers and sisters around every day. I can tell you're happy, Mom and Dad, that I'm getting my license, because now you'll be off the hook for swim lessons, orthodontist appointments, and detentions. Well, I'm not ready to spend my afternoons and weekends doing that!"

If that's the meaning Meredith's parents interpret from her behavior, they might sit down and talk over the situation with each other first, then discuss with Meredith what the "chauffeur" schedule will be like after the driver's test. She will not be asked to turn, in one terrible moment, into a full-time caregiver for her brothers and sisters.

Once again, obviously no single response is "right." However, there *is* a single *wrong* response, and that is to react as if your child deliberately set out to wreck your car, raise your insurance rates, and ruin your life. Her little spin was not directed toward you; you were not the target. Her accident had a deeper meaning that was directed outward from herself and based in her struggle for independence and identity. It is your task as a POA to assess the situation calmly—no matter how dire it seems—and then, taking cues from the child you know so well, to order *your* behavior so that she can re-order hers, based upon your measured, structured responses.

Yet another example, this one fairly serious, illustrates the need to set strict parameters once you have understood the meaning behind your adolescent's behavior.

Your 15-year-old daughter Leah is the premier babysitter in town. She is usually employed both Friday and Saturday nights, and frequently one or two evenings during the week. You are very proud of her, and of her extremely responsible behavior. Parents love her, even fight over her, because their children love her and clamor for her. She plays with them, gets their teeth brushed, sees that they're in bed on time. She goes so far as to help straighten the house once the kids are asleep. In addition to being punctual, conscientious, and peppy, she doesn't even eat a lot. You look forward to chatting with your neighbors, because somehow the talk always turns to Leah and her fantastic babysitting prowess.

One day you hear some disquieting news. Several items—bracelets, rings, perfume—have disappeared from three homes after Leah has been there. You find yourself coming up with explanations to yourself that scream "coincidence," and will hear of no connection between Leah and the missing objects. You are sure that the items will soon reappear, with no relationship to Leah at all. Soon, however, before you've had a chance to figure out what to say (if anything), Leah appears at the Barnetts' house to babysit —wearing Mrs. Barnett's earrings.

Once again, your natural reaction is to see this behavior in terms of what it means to you: Your daughter, who is not only a thief but also a fairly inept one, has humiliated you in front of the entire community. You might want to scream at her and call her a jerk; you might even threaten to go to the police, in order to teach her that famous lesson she'll "never forget"; you might lay a major league guilt trip on her, highlighting her betrayal of the Barnetts' trust in her ("They even brought you that jewelry box from China!"), wondering rhetorically how you or anyone else in town can ever trust her again, and finishing up by asking, "Is there anything else you've stolen that we should know about?"

Those born-in-the-gut, shot-from-the-hip responses would certainly send Leah your message of wrath, disappointment, and mortification, but they would do nothing to address the more important, less clear issue of what she meant by her hapless stealing spree. If you are able to remove yourself from the immediacy of Leah's plight—if you can picture yourself in the role of a nonjudgmental new neighbor, rather than as the chagrined parent of a pilfering teenage girl—you might see that Leah's actions were not simply spiteful or bone-headed. Any person who revisits the scene of a crime wearing evidence of that crime obviously hopes to be caught, and gives you the opportunity to play the "good cop," rather than the "bad cop." You need to discover why your daughter acted so rashly. You, as a POA, must zero in on the meaning of her behavior, rather than permit yourself the luxury of simply reacting as a hurt and angry parent and punishing her without mercy for stealing.

This may be a way for Leah to say, "Get me out of this! Everyone expects me to be so competent, so mature, so perfect, but I'm only 15 years old! I hate being cooped up in a house with little kids and big responsibilities. I'd love to be out with my friends on weekends, but instead I've got to babysit, because everyone depends on me. Help!"

By observing that Leah is behaving in a way no truly mature person would, you comprehend much about the meaning of her behavior. Now, however, you must go even further and decide what to do about this obvious call for help.

Are you able to solve the problem at its source, perhaps by suggesting that she earn her money not by babysitting, but by working at a frozen yogurt stand where she would have less responsibility *and* be able to see her friends? Or is this a situation you feel incapable of dealing with yourself? You might very well know Leah's catch-me behavior is odd, but be unable to decipher it, or you may understand what the behavior means, yet not really know how to handle it or what the next step should be.

There's nothing wrong with feeling that way. Nowhere is it written that POAs must have all the answers—or even know all the questions. It is a sign of strength, not weakness, to admit that in certain situations the help of a therapist or other counselor is needed. By recognizing Leah's behavior as an awkward cry for help, rather than as an "in your face" slap at all you hold dear, you have already initiated the process of supplying that aid.

Leah's behavior is wild, messy, out of bounds. That's why it's so important for you to walk quietly away for a moment—against all your instincts that tell you to wade in and flail away. Only by assessing this unstructured, unclear behavior from a calm, measured, "across the street" perspective can you provide your adolescent with the clarity and order she so desperately needs.

Another form of taking behavior personally is to blame yourself for what happened. This can take many shapes: You may ask repeatedly what you might have done to lead to this behavior, or you may resolve dramatically to change your style of discipline.

Do not do that. By focusing on your own behavior and your intense self-doubt, you may be removing energy from understanding the meaning behind Leah's behavior. Further, and perhaps more deleterious, you may not get Leah the professional help she genuinely needs for this serious act.

A SIGNAL FOR PROFESSIONAL HELP

Good parents do not stop being good parents if they decide their adolescent needs professional help. Sometimes the situation is too muddled to make clear sense of, no matter how hard you try.

Your son Paul is 14 years old. He badgers you all winter long to spend the summer at a camp his friends have told him about, where he can be part of the oldest group. He reviews the camp literature, including a videotape of the daily program, and seems enthusiastic about the eight-week session. Although he has attended other camps in previous summers, with mixed reviews, he insists this one is different. "They understand teenagers and how we don't want to have a bunch of boring rules," he says. "Sports are voluntary, and we're not forced to play basketball every day at ten." Paul convinces you of the validity of his position; you send in your tuition, buy him camp clothes, and send him off with good wishes for a great summer and a stack of pre-addressed postcards.

But before three weeks pass, you receive four telephone calls from the camp director concerning Paul's behavior. During the first call, you find out that Paul is staying in the cabin for hours at a time listening to his Walkman, refusing to participate in any activities. A few days later the director informs you of Paul's rude and verbally abusive behavior to several counselors when they tell him he cannot get into a canoe without a life jacket—and without the paddles either. You are next told about Paul's early morning departure from his cabin to raid the kitchen for food (while smoking cigarettes). The last phone call details his serious defiance of safety rules at the swimming pool in front of many younger campers.

The final call comes the next week, and it is Paul's exit notice from camp: He has stolen some money from bunkmates and counselors. Sadly, and with great confusion, you arrange for Paul and his trunk to be sent home. At this point, you take the requisite step back and attempt mightily to interpret the meaning of his behavior—but your efforts fail.

It is here that a therapist is needed to slice through the mixed messages. Perhaps Paul is torn between conflicting emotions: wanting to leave home and be independent (my parents are a burden), and feeling dependent on his family and familiar surroundings (my parents need me and I need them). Perhaps he was genuinely misled by the camp literature, and he found that the authority he was struggling with in the parental relationship was also present in the camp setting. Whatever the answer, the meaning of Paul's behavior is multifaceted, and it may take a professional quite a bit of time to help Paul figure out the true meaning of his behavior.

Although behavior such as Paul's may appear confusing, even contradictory, it usually is not indecipherable. Every action your adolescent makes, every pose he adopts, every mood he reflects, has a reason. We are not advising you to push, probe and pry into his life to determine why he slouches one day, struts the next, slinks the third. An adolescent, like anyone else, has a right to privacy. Besides, if you try to find the meaning behind every single behavior pattern, you'll be a good candidate for observation yourself.

However, at certain times in your life as a POA—the day your son decides not to play football; the evening your daughter mows down the mailbox; the afternoon the neighbors gossip about the light-fingered babysitter—you will be tempted to march into your adolescent's room angrily, your eyes ablaze as you tear down the don't-look-back track.

It is at those times that prudent POAs take a step back, close their eyes, and silence their tongues. They count to ten—100, if need be—and turn away from their difficult teenager. They look instead, inside themselves. They check their own values and look for creative interpretations until they find the correct one(s) that fit their child. They allow time to order their behavior, so that their youngster can explore the meaning of his actions with them and order his own behavior. And then, finally, they come up with meaningful structures and boundaries that are appropriate to that meaning.

That's the theory, anyway. The next nine chapters will discuss specific types of adolescent behavior, from mood swings to sexual practices and give you a chance to think about our advice to POAs:

Remember that all behavior has meaning.

Remember that meaning comes from your adolescent's search for values.

Remember that the way to assist in that search is to set limits on behavior.

4 | "Testing the Limits" Behavior: Who's in Charge Here?

Being the parent of an adolescent is in many ways a positive experience. It is an exciting opportunity to participate in the shaping and molding of a nascent personality into an integrated, defined human being. It is also a uniquely challenging period for you and your child. But let's face it, adolescence may also be more like an itch you can't scratch—an itch that your adolescent is constantly and deliberately attempting to make you scratch.

Life with an adolescent is often defined not in terms of major crises—car wrecks, drug addiction, pregnancies—but in terms of niggling irritations: messy bathrooms, unfilled gas tanks, permanently attached Walkmen. We all live our lives on a day-to-day, somewhat routine basis. Everyone has daily chores and responsibilities, including teenagers, and there are often very real consequences to a lack of order.

Monica fails to put her soiled laundry into the hamper, thereby missing the wash on Thursday and sowing the seeds for a minor panic attack on Friday morning as she prepares for school and discovers no clean underwear in her drawer. Tom's neglect of the garbage for a day is not only an inconvenience when the pail overflows but also leads to an army of ants on the scene the next morning, with everyone missing breakfast to deal with the problem. An open can of half-used dog food sits on the refrigerator shelf, next to the pie you're saving for weekend company. An empty tube of Jackie's acne medication sits on her bathroom table early Saturday evening; her high-pitched shriek echoes throughout the house when she discovers she's out of salve. Bob dresses for the school dance, and as he puts on the "right" pants he discovers the large rip that he did, in fact, know of, but neglected to mention to you or take care of himself.

Taken separately, these are insignificant distractions. But add them up, as any POA is forced to, and they become immense, troublesome obstacles to the sane functioning of the family unit. By and large, it is these minor "itches," annoying by themselves, overpowering when taken together, that make adolescence such a tricky rash to treat.

But treat it you can. The key is to set limits on the behavior. These limits derive from understanding the values by which you want your family to live, and by which you want to define the boundaries of your adolescent's behavior. Your goal is to get your adolescent to accept the limits you set; to integrate them into individual behaviors and actions.

While it is important that your values and boundaries must be clear to your adolescent, it is important to realize that values and boundaries are different. Values should remain constant, while boundaries may be flexible (so long as that flexibility does not betray your family values).

For example, let's say your family values good health. It follows that to be in good health, everyone needs adequate sleep—and it follows from that that your adolescents have a weekend curfew. That is your value, but because your boundaries can be flexible, there is no problem with extending that curfew for special occasions, just as there is no problem reconsidering the curfew hour at the start of each school year. Your boundaries stretch as your adolescents grow—but your values should not shift.

Let's say you also value a sense of the family as a unit and want to communicate that value to your children. There may have been regular breakfast and dinner meals when they were younger; that was one way in which this value was lived. There could well have been family outings every couple of weeks, and some longer vacation excursions. At holiday time, your home served as a center for larger extended family gatherings.

Now that your children are adolescents and have become more involved in their own separate pursuits, it may be necessary to alter the family meal schedule, the trip policy, and the holiday traditions. It may well be that a meal at a special restaurant, a family discussion of a significant television show, or attendance at a school play or athletic event will now become the avenues for expressing the "family as a unit" value. Once again, boundaries change, but values remain constant.

Ah, but let's go back once more to our "adolescent itch." Remember, we said that your adolescent wants to make you scratch. In fact, just as it is the POA's job to set boundaries, so too is it the adolescent's job to test the parameters. It is a function of adolescence—it's written into the genes, right next to "hormone explosion" and "insatiable appetite"—to challenge limits.

And so you are faced with the unenviable task of easing your adolescent-borne itch *without* scratching. When your daughter makes a rude comment, she wants you to respond in kind; when your son sticks his nose right up against yours, he'd love you to go head to head. That's all part of the great adolescent challenge.

But for you to snipe or spar is to limit the power of the very limits you're attempting to set. That's the Clint Eastwood model: "Go ahead, make my day." Instead, you should emulate Kenny Rogers and his gambler: "You've got to know when to hold 'em; know when to fold 'em; know when to walk away, know when to . . ."—well, not run exactly, but you get the idea. You've got to be calmer, more thoughtful, and analytical than your adolescent. That's the only way you can set limits and make them stick, because your adolescent is going to challenge your limits, and not all of them should be inflexible.

Adolescents need room to learn not only how to accept limits but also how to compromise and adjust their own behavior, while still feeling in control of themselves and of their situation. They can't do that if every limit they face is inviolable, and if the limits seem to be set arbitrarily. That's why your boundaries must be consistent with your values, creative and, in some cases, flexible—though they must never be insecure.

But enough talk. Let's take a look at the Roland family to show what we mean.

Al Roland, the father of this solidly middle class suburban family, is the 45-year-old sales manager for a soft drink bottling company. His wife, Jo Ellen, is 42; she went back to work eight years ago and is now the art director at a small advertising agency.

Melissa, 17, and her brother Chris, 14, are above average students at their high school; they've never presented any problems there or at summer camp. Melissa plays basketball, sings in the choir, and is a member of Students Against Drunk Driving. Chris is on the junior varsity soccer and varsity ski teams, and has recently become interested in photography. Both children are active in the local church group.

Melissa and Chris are seen by the outside world as nice, responsible kids, just as the Roland family is viewed as a secure, stable unit. Inside the home, things are a lot less Cleaverish. Life has become perhaps not unhappy but certainly uncomfortable, for many reasons.

For instance, Jo Ellen has started to dread coming home at 5:30, because she knows she'll walk into a less welcoming environment than she needs after a stressful day at work. Although she'll have straightened the house up quickly before leaving in the morning, the kitchen will show signs of combat: half-filled glasses in the sink, ice cream stains on the counter, school books strewn across the table. The television set will be on, although no one will be in the den, and music will pound from both the basement and the upstairs bedrooms. It's not that Melissa and Chris don't know the boundaries of proper behavior; they've had limits set before, and they continue to ignore them.

Jo Ellen anticipates her entrance into her somewhat less than ordered (and intolerably noisy) home, and wonders how she'll deal with it. She has previously felt annoyed, unappreciated, sad, frustrated and taken advantage of, to mention just a few feelings. She is certain that she adores both children, is well aware that they are basically decent, caring young adults, yet the negative feelings she has transcend all else the moment she walks through the side door.

Al arrives half an hour later, often tired from managing people and product problems at work. His day is usually laden with sales personnel who fail to file reports on time, dissatisfied customers who blast salespeople for false promises or rude behavior, and a boss who wants to know things like why sales have lagged by 20 percent in zone 6 this week. Al is hoping for a bit of respite from the drain on his emotional energy after handling crisis after crisis, and is therefore disheartened to open the door to a loud "Dammit Mom, you never understand anyway," delivered in less than loving tones by Melissa.

"Dinner!" Jo Ellen tries her best to keep the call light and upbeat as she yells above the other sounds in the house to summon everyone to the evening meal. This used to be a wonderfully calm half hour, with easy communication, some sense of respect for the others at the table, even some participation in clearing and dishwashing. Now both Melissa and Chris bolt down their food to get to the demands of their busy teenage evening schedules.

They come to the table predictably garbed: Melissa in a marginally obscene t-shirt, Chris with a turned-around baseball cap; neither wears shoes or socks. Their dress is just inappropriate enough to be annoying, just appropriate enough for their parents to ignore.

Conversations are usually punctuated with some less-than-amicable personal exchanges between Chris and Melissa:

"You're such a dweeb. I can't believe you said that, moron."

"You mean you're only getting to that unit now? God, we had that the first week of school."

"Typical. Your musical taste is about at the level of my first grade hamster."

"Try deodorant or a shower. They help."

"Mom, Dad, do I have to sit here and listen to that crap?"

When Jo Ellen and Al attempt to discuss the events at work or to inquire about school, they are often interrupted by something like, "Oh yeah, I need $40 for lab fees for dissection. If I don't bring it in tomorrow, I'll flunk."

Following dinner, weekday evenings at the Rolands usually involve a steady increase in decibels, back to pre-dinner levels. The telephone rings incessantly. Despite having purchased most of the "conveniences" offered by the phone company (a separate children's line, Totalphone, extensions in nearly every room), the parents can never seem to get to the few calls they must make, either business or personal. Furthermore, the call never seems to be for the person who answers the phone, which leads to great shouting matches between rooms. ("Melissa—it's you-know-who *again!*" must be yelled, in order to be heard above the rock concerts emanating from both teenagers' rooms.).

And, of course, there is a fair amount of bickering over the length and importance of each conversation. "You just talked to her ten minutes ago. Clothes designs and hairstyles don't change that quickly," is a typical Chris comment, while the rejoinder might be, "At least I get called for something besides homework. You spent forty minutes discussing algebra and some stupid sign properties, whatever that is."

In general homework appears to be a low priority, although whenever Jo Ellen asks Chris to take out the garbage, he promises to do it "later, Mom. I'm on the phone. I gotta find out about this lab report." Although the garbage— and walking Taffy, the dog—are nominally the kids' responsibilities, in reality the parents often end up doing them, because—well, who knows, just because.

The evening concludes in relative peace, although the kids go to bed later than Al and Jo Ellen would like, and the post-10:30 phone calls are irksome. But it's the morning that brings *sturm und drang*. Both adolescents own clock radios that are mechanically flawless, but somehow Melissa and Chris fail to respond to them. Jo Ellen thus wins the task of rousing two grumpy teenagers, along with fixing breakfast for four and preparing for work herself.

The wakeup routine is familiar to everyone with teenagers. "Mom, I know the alarm went off, I'm using the snooze button. I'm not six years old. I'll be up in five minutes, I promise" alternates with "How could you let me oversleep? You know that clock never works. Didn't you not hear me getting dressed?," with an occasional "If you bought me a car, I'd take my dumb brother to school and then we could all sleep later instead of this ridiculous wakeup nonsense" thrown in.

Of course, for Melissa certainly (and perhaps for Chris), finding the right clothes is not easy. There is the unanticipated change in the weather, or the suddenly remembered after school club meeting with the cute boy Melissa wants to impress (in which case she tries on seven outfits before saying to Jo Ellen in exasperation, "I have absolutely nothing to wear. I need your purple jump suit, Mom. Please, it's just for today!") On bad days a large portion of Jo Ellen's wardrobe may be found in Melissa's closet (or, more likely, on her floor). And if this isn't irritating enough, Jo Ellen has on occasion spotted some of her favorite sweaters being worn by Melissa's friends.

Complicating the busy morning routine may well be the quick breakfast communication from Melissa: "Mom, I don't know when I'll be home today. I have a meeting at school and then Sharon and I are going to the mall together and then to study. So don't worry about dinner."

Jo Ellen weakly attempts to get some details about the plan, to ask for a call at her office when Melissa knows definitely what time she'll be home, but her voice disappears in the air as Melissa hastily departs, papers falling out of her backpack, and her purse still on the counter.

Chris, on the other hand, has no idea where to find his loose-leaf notebook with all of his assignments. While his parents are searching for the binder, he announces proudly, "Dad, I got a job delivering phone books. I need you to help me this weekend, but I'm going to do most of it on my bike this week. The books aren't that heavy, so I'll only need your help with the car Friday night, Saturday, and maybe Sunday."

As Al tries to question him about age requirements, the need for some kind of work permit, and details about how much and when he'll be paid, Chris dismisses him quickly. "Kevin knows all that, Dad. Don't worry about it." Before that instant, Al has never heard Kevin's name. Thus begins a typical weekday in the Roland household.

On weekends, the irritations are different; from Friday night to Sunday the issues change. On Friday Chris rushes from the dinner table at 6:10 even more precipitously than usual, announcing that he needs a ride to his friend Benjie's. The entire soccer team was supposed to be there at six to celebrate their victory over their archrival the previous afternoon. No, he doesn't know if Benjie's parents will be home, and what difference does that make anyway, and can he *please* not have to be home at the regular 11:30 curfew so he doesn't look like a total dork in front of his friends?

In the meantime, Melissa enumerates, in her machine-gun fashion, the following: "I'll be staying overnight at Charlene's tonight, then I'm going directly to basketball practice tomorrow morning, then I have to have the car around noon to pick up Holly and Jennifer 'cause we're rehearsing our solo for the choir. And you can't insist that I get home tomorrow before midnight, since you know we're trying to get that Students Against Drunk Driving resolution passed to allow us to get into designated driver and safe rides programs. And we've got to have a *little* time for fun after that, right?"

Al and Jo Ellen's attempts to introduce topics like lawn mowing, homework, and room straightening are met first with stares of astonishment, then verbal protestations that these responsibilities will, of course, be met (no problem!). The general climate is one of loud confusion and protest. The additional complication of whether Chris should play soccer or be available for dinner with his grandparents late Sunday afternoon is unresolved. It is interrupted in mid-yell and then forgotten about as Chris rushes off to the party at Benjie's.

In short, the Roland house is in the throes of adolescence, with stress permeating the relationships among all four family members. These two teenagers are engaging in that absolutely predictable adolescent game, "Testing the Limits." It's often not dramatic or destructive; it's simply a constant pushing and pulling at the boundaries of what is expected.

Limits have been set by the parents, often with the participation of the adolescent, and each teenager is driven to discover which boundaries are for real and which have some flexibility. When the Roland children were younger, home was a relatively ordered, predictable, safe place for everyone to be. Chris and Melissa basically followed the rules, wanting to please their parents and garner their approval. At the developmental stage of preadolescence, identity was defined very much by going along with rules.

Today, Chris and Melissa are trying to find themselves by straining against limits and boundaries. As the limit-testing proceeds, Al and Jo Ellen are often uncomfortable and vaguely dissatisfied. Yet the issues are neither sharp nor clear nor are they of any magnitude. So the problems may go unattended or only partially addressed, and the Rolands remain a somewhat unhappy, uncomfortable family.

Does your family life resemble the Roland household?

All of us lead more or less fragmented lives; our families don't always click together on all cylinders, and at different times different people in our households will have different—sometimes conflicting—interests, needs, and priorities. That's a fact of American life in the 1990s.

Obviously, you cannot address every single issue of adolescence. First, to find enough time, you would have to forgo all other jobs and activities—and to find enough patience and wisdom, you would have to become a saint.

Second, adolescents such as Chris and Melissa *need* to have limits they can test. By doing so, they can find out that they are powerful individuals; that they do exert some control over themselves and their world, and that discovery is just as vital as learning that there are limits they cannot change.

It's important to remember that if you react to every issue, you are making a fundamental error. You are placing all adolescent behavior on the same, equal plane. It isn't all equal. Certain behaviors are worth making an issue over; others are not. You cannot possibly monitor, address, and solve every adolescent action that bothers you—so don't even try. Certain annoying behavior must be allowed. If you nitpick every action, your home will become a war zone, and just as bad, your adolescent will be unable to differentiate between serious and trivial issues.

Yet you must set limits on issues you feel are important. There are no laundry lists: Issues to Deal With; Issues to Avoid. Some behaviors that you deem critical may seem irrelevant to your friends or neighbors, and vice versa. That's okay; that's where your values come in. It's not the issues we are concerned with here, but rather *why* you choose to deal with them.

The way in which you select your issues should be reasonable and straightforward, not indirect and haphazard. Your choice of issues should be based on your values. If you feel that some particular adolescent behavior is destructive, or offensive to a value you feel is important to your family, then you must address the behavior.

Of course, each family has the obligation to define its own values and the types of value definition will vary: In one family importance may be attached to physical activity or competitive sports, in another it may be playing music, reading, or the pursuit of academic excellence; in yet another it may be learning a trade or participation in the family business from an early age.

Then there are those values that are defined societally, which means they have taken on ethical and legal overtones and have broader implications than the challenge of individual family values. Theft and promiscuity are examples of serious violations of legal and moral standards. Underage teenage driving and the purchase and distribution of alcohol are also limit-crossing behaviors. These are all serious values that deserve *everyone's* attention.

How does this value-setting process work? First, it should begin well before behavior reaches the crisis stage. It is much easier to think, talk, and plan when events are not swirling around us—which is why discussions or thoughts about values should be part of an ongoing, rather than an intermittent, process.

Second, any discussion of values between parents must be done in private, away from the aggravating adolescent. This can take the form of a "bathroom conference" with your spouse, dinner together, or even a weekend away from home. (If you are divorced, and for whatever reason you and your ex are unable to meet face to face, this process can be accomplished by phone.) These discussions are a good time to raise issues and problems that are of obvious concern but may seem too broad, complex, or difficult to discuss during the hectic, day-to-day activities of the typical American family.

During these discussions, you should agree not to react reflexively to your adolescent's behavior; rather, you should look at the meaning of the behavior and decide rationally which behavior is not that big a deal and is thus worth giving in on (which allows adolescents room to test themselves). You should then identify behavior that violates your values and thus demands that boundaries be set.

Through a series of such rational parental discussions, you might determine that your son's boundaries are different than your daughter's, or that what is working today might not work six months from now, when you've got two teenage drivers, not one.

You might decide that a messy room does not really violate any important values, no matter how aesthetically unpleasing it is. Your solution might be to tell your son that if he chooses not to clean his room, then he must keep his door shut. He must also agree not to have any food in his room, because you don't want to witness the creation of any new life forms.

You might conclude that the problem of borrowing clothes can be solved simply by having your daughter *ask* you for whatever she'd like. The issue, you might see, is not one of borrowing per se, but of your resentment of her lack of consideration for you, which she demonstrates by not asking your permission.

You might feel that while it is an important value for all family members to have chores, your method of assigning them causes friction. One solution would be to make a list of jobs, then sit down with your children and work out a flexible schedule that's agreeable to all concerned.

Regarding curfews, you might decide that this is one value that requires strict limits. You must also realize this is an issue all adolescents feel strongly about (because of peer pressure, the need for independence, and a youthful urge to carouse when every oldster is abed). Let's suppose you are talking to your daughter about your concerns.

"Your father and I understand some families are comfortable without curfews," you might begin. "But we need to sleep, and we can't do that if you're out—even if we know where you are." The curfew thus becomes a limit. You can *involve* your daughter in the precise time limit that gets set, through negotiation and compromise (these are important skills for any youngster to learn), but you should know ahead of time what your own, inviolate limits are.

If your daughter says, "Well, I guess 2 A.M. is okay with me," feel free to say, "Well, it's not okay with me. I need more sleep than that. And I can't fall asleep until you're home."

The old '60s saying, "If you're not part of the solution, you're part of the problem," remains true in the '90s. It is important that your adolescent see herself as part of the solution, and you can help her do that by delivering the solution to a problem not as an arbitrary rule, but as an agreement worked out between mature, reasonable people. By delivering an arbitrary rule, you encourage impulsive behavior; arbitrarily is how an adolescent acts, and you don't want to act as an adolescent does—not when you're trying to help an adolescent order her life. By providing order, you're helping establish that order in your adolescent's own life.

But, of course, rules will be broken; established limits will be breached. This is not, after all, Fantasyland or Mayberry R.F.D. One night your daughter will stroll in not at 11:59, but at 1:59, and you will be wide awake, even angrier than you'd be had you simply set a curfew without having that "mature, reasonable" conversation. What do you do when a rule you considered inviolate is, in fact, violated?

As a POA, you must know that you and your limits will always be tested. So you must prepare yourself for violations before they occur. You can't afford to be surprised when the limits you've set are pushed, stretched, or broken (although it is a basic rule of POAhood that this must happen at the worst possible time, and when you least expect it). By being prepared, you'll be better able to avoid the natural impulse to shriek, and can instead ask yourself: What is the meaning of this behavior? Why did it happen? What value is being transgressed?

One meaning could be that she is *only* limit-testing—asking, "Is this boundary for real? Who's in charge here, me or my parents? Is this one of those rules that they really mean business about, and therefore around which I have no room to challenge?"

Another meaning could be that in addition to limit-testing she is exploring her sexuality, having her first intimate experience with her new boyfriend, quite unaware of the passage of time—or very aware, and consciously deciding to pursue a degree of sexual intimacy nevertheless. Or she may be testing her mind by having her first discussion of deep questions, such as the meaning of life and mortality, or career versus motherhood, with her old girlfriends.

You're mad and you're scared, but you've got to take that deep breath; you must step back and find out all the facts, or as many of them as you can. It is possible, indeed probable, that you know your adolescent better than anyone; you know which facial expressions or gestures make it plain that she is telling the truth, and conversely those clues that indicate she is bending the truth, "forgetting" certain details. You'll instinctively know as a POA how to discern when she's been up to no good, when circumstances have simply conspired against her, and when she has in fact been out exploring and testing in a benign fashion.

With all of the above considerations in mind, and at least some of the data at hand based on your daughter's recitation of why she came in two hours past curfew, you can say, "Honey, it's 2 A.M. You broke the rule. Earlier, I was worried; now I'm just tired. I'm beyond mad. I'm going to bed. You can, too, but you don't have to; you can stay up and think about it—because we're going to talk about it in the morning."

By speaking those words as calmly as you can, you acknowledge that a rule has been broken, a line has been crossed, but your reaction is neither hasty nor spiteful. You set up a waiting period, an extended version of the deep breath that prevents unnecessary tension, precludes impudent words, or regrettable deeds. You also leave some room for your adolescent to think through her behavior, to evaluate what she has done in the relatively emotion-free setting of her own room by herself, not in the presence of a tired, distraught parent. The additional positive message you send your teenager concerns the importance of making considered decisions, rather than issuing impulsive, arbitrary orders.

In the morning when you're semi-rested, and the waiting period is over, you and your daughter sit down to a breakfast she has guiltily prepared. You have a tremendous opportunity to get her to agree that a boundary has been crossed, to go over again the rationale for the existence of that boundary, and to ask your adolescent what your reaction should be.

Note that the question is *not* what "the punishment" should be. Adolescents are too old to be "punished," but they are certainly not too old to understand the concept of "consequences," and to realize that when they test certain limits, they run the risk of suffering certain consequences.

And the consequences should be directly related to the limit-testing behavior. Abuse of phone privileges should not result in curtailment of curfew but in curtailment of the right to use the phone. All behavior has meaning, and limit-testing behavior has consequences that are directly related to the behavior itself.

It is important for your daughter to understand the difference between punishment and consequences. The former is imposed by an outside agent; the latter is something she brings upon herself. By setting limits and reacting to those limits when they are violated, you can send a direct message to your adolescent that actions have consequences, and that she is responsible for any unwanted consequences she brings upon herself. By learning this, your daughter learns a valuable lesson about the importance of ordering her own behavior.

But she cannot learn that lesson unless your response is rational, measured, and clear. Chances are it won't be, unless you have already spent time ordering and understanding your own behavior. This is done not by acting impulsively, but by taking as much time as is needed in an inflammatory situation to assess, analyze, and react to whatever circumstance is occurring. Each transgression presents an opportunity to have a full, frank, and dynamic parent/ teenager discussion. (Each situation also represents a unique set of circumstances for parents and adolescents, and that is why limits should not be set in advance.)

Now, if your daughter is like most adolescent curfew violators we know, she won't like it when you tell her that the consequence of her behavior is that she will stay home next weekend. "You're punishing me!" she'll squawk.

"No," you'll reply. "You brought this on yourself with your own behavior. We didn't take away next weekend; you did."

Your words are crisp, your message clear. You are saying: All behavior has meaning and consequences. Your job is to get your adolescent to understand that simple fact—and to accept the limits you've agreed to; to adopt them, and to integrate them into her own behavior and actions. If you can do that, then your home, unlike the Rolands', will become a place where family values are clear, consistent, and concrete, and which you and your adolescent share and enjoy together.

5 | **F**ads and Friends

Anyone who has lived with a teenager for any length of time knows that the peer group assumes an inordinate importance during adolescence. Like it or not, what your adolescent's friends think, say, and do is vastly more important to him than what you, your spouse, or any other adult thinks, says, or does. In fact, it is often more critical than what he himself thinks, says, or does.

Winning the respect of the peer group, and the attendant sense of belonging to a large community of other teenagers, is so crucial to some adolescents that it may cause them to lose all perspective on anything else. The desire to be part of a group, to adopt their peers' style of dress, type of diet, pattern of speech, may overwhelm all other functioning aspects of this heretofore well-groomed, health conscious, articulate teenager.

And that's not necessarily bad. Although the immediate result is aggravating—who among us is honestly not thrown by seeing boxer shorts worn as a fashion statement, watching Pepsi drunk as a breakfast drink, or hearing "like" used as the most common word in the English language?—the underlying motivation for such behavior is understandable. Through outlandish dress, behavior, or speech that is shared with many others of their own age and no one else in the world, adolescents are experimenting with divergent values. And that's part of the task of adolescence. They are straining against the boundaries you as a POA have set for them. Again, your task is to hold strong to your values so that your teenager will know and understand that they are important and meaningful.

Here's a little secret: Most adolescents might not even *like* all the fads they're experimenting with. They may feel embarrassed wearing a tank top, hungry without meat in their diet, stupid when they hear themselves speak "teen talk," but the urge to be accepted by their peers is so overpowering that they'll endure those feelings. That's entirely appropriate.

It's difficult but soothing to realize that fads don't last forever. Today's safety pins give way to tomorrow's earrings; the computer game nut becomes, in time, a chess or bridge player. Your child will not wear weird clothing or speak in bizarre tongues forever; a fad by its very nature is transitory, ephemeral, even laughable. In your bleakest moments, take heart from what you observe all around you. The number of your friends who still wear bell-bottoms, drive VW micro-buses, and say "groovy" and "far out" is probably small indeed.

Throughout history, there has never been a time when adolescents have *not* used fads as a means of sparking their parents' interest in them. Take perhaps the most visible fad of all: dress. One year it was flappers, then came bobby socks, then miniskirts. Today adolescents might wear oversized shirts, tomorrow—the mind shudders.

Do we *agree* with every changing fashion; do we find them all attractive, interesting, or appealing? Of course not. But—far more important—we also must ask ourselves: Is it destructive? Does a certain style of dress, type of jewelry, or method of lacing shoes actually harm anyone? Once again, of course not.

In fact, most fads are not only not *de*structive but actually *con*structive in purpose. They allow adolescents a two-pronged opportunity: to rebel against their parents (and test their own developing values by seeking limits), while simultaneously banding together with a group that provides them with support in that same search for identity.

What seems "abnormal" behavior to parents is, in fact, "normal" to adolescents. Distasteful or unlikable, maybe—perhaps even dyspepsia-producing—but normal nonetheless. For the most part, fads are a safe way for teenagers to test their (and your) limits.

Let's say your son invests an inordinate amount of energy in spiking his hair. He spends his hard-earned money on all manner of spike goo; he rises early to commandeer prime bathroom time; he even forgoes breakfast in order to make sure each follicle stands up just so.

You, on the other hand, have always preached that breakfast is the most important meal of the day; you wish he would get a bit more sleep, and note with dismay that he looks like a porcupine whenever he emerges from his hour-long ritual.

But is spiked hair a hill worth dying on? Is it a battle you should spend time and energy fighting? And if you deliver an ultimatum—"You're not leaving the house like that, young man!"—how, realistically, can you ever enforce it? How can you avoid the confrontation? ("I'm at the door! Try to stop me!" "You'll never touch that car again!" "I've got the keys!")

This is truly a no-win situation. Adolescents know it is difficult for you to follow through on threats made in haste, anger, or frustration; they know impulsive statements when they hear them. These are the kinds of behavior we want adolescents to learn to monitor in themselves. And when spoken by parents trying to regain power through might, they are doomed to failure, because they are threats made from weakness, not judgments made from strength.

Far better to maintain your sense of humor about such situations. If you can view them objectively, they actually become funny: A boy who previously showed absolutely no interest in any form of grooming now spends upward of an hour each morning making himself appear like a cartoon character, in the name of individuality. All his friends perform the same ritual. They earnestly think they look good (or pretend that they do).

The situation is a truly humorous one. So your best recourse is to try to keep your perspective and have faith that this perfectly appropriate adolescent behavior will eventually abate. Chances are very good that your son will not walk down the aisle to wed his wife with his hair looking like something out of a tropical rain forest.

A side note: It is, we know, difficult to continually serve as an "ordering force" in our adolescents' lives when each of us, as POAs, still has a bit of unresolved adolescent in us. As our children thumb their noses at society and its conventions by dressing, acting, and talking "unconventionally," who among us does not wish to do the same from time to time?

(Admit it: We've all harbored the dream of walking into the office in jeans, or blurting out in the middle of a dull cocktail party exactly how we feel. But, for better or worse, we are all grown-ups in a grown-up world, and our adolescents want us to remain that way and to serve as a strong, ordering force for them. An adolescent's job, we have mentioned before, is to test limits; a POA's job is to maintain the base that allows them their safe tests.)

Things had been going very well in the Simmons household until Becky, the second child, turned 15. Oldest daughter Sandi was preparing to go off to college, having just completed a productive four years of high school. Becky had recently begun to make strongly rebellious statements—strong enough, in fact, to more than make up for her sister's apparently easy slide through adolescence.

Becky loved the mall. She could (and did) spend hours each week hanging out there with her friends. It got to the point that she regularly spent more hours there than at home and school, and naturally her grades and family relationships began to suffer. She claimed that she was meeting lots of interesting people from lots of interesting schools at the mall and went so far as to describe herself as a "goodwill ambassador."

Meanwhile her parents had great difficulty understanding this phenomenon. The stark contrast between Sandi and Becky befuddled them; they felt so sure they had been fair, loving, and supportive to both girls. They could always talk to Sandi, and she to them, about anything. With Becky, they just were not sure.

They had reservations about all the time Becky spent at the mall but hoped it was a phase that would pass. Because they felt that confronting Becky would not be productive, they continued to "wait and see." As time passed there was a slow shift in attire, as Becky progressed into clothing that was more and more outrageous and provocative. Again, they felt that this was a personal statement and they were not sure about how to confront it.

When Becky began to stop asking her parents to drive her to the mall (her friends would take her), they seemed a bit relieved. But when she began being dropped off at home by boys they had never met or even seen, their concerns grew. One night they were called to pick up Becky in a neighboring town. She had been in an automobile accident; luckily, no one was injured.

This was the incident the Simmonses could no longer ignore. They had been pushed to the limits of their boundaries, but they did not know what steps lay ahead. Becky did not think there was any problem—certainly there was no reason to be punished. She was thus not going to help directly in any solution. It was up to the parents to decide alone what was going to happen (knowing full well that Becky was not going to be happy about it).

Before confronting Becky, the parents talked alone about their values versus their desires for Becky. They tried to separate the two and to work together to define their values, which they then presented to their daughter. They told her she could still go to the mall with her friends, but the time would be curtailed. Although they wished that she would go there only to shop, they knew that she went there because this was where her social life was centered. They also knew that Becky would be filled with resentment if she were kept home.

They next faced the issue of Becky's clothes. Again, although they wished that Becky would dress like Sandi, they recognized the fact that Becky was not Sandi. They had a long discussion about "clothes that make statements about individuality" as opposed to "clothes that make statements about loose sexual values." The Simmonses were not a prudish family, but neither were they without certain moral standards.

Finally, they addressed the issues of cars, boys, and knowing Becky's whereabouts. Their first concern involved their desire to know where Becky was going when she left the house. This, they explained, would make them feel comfortable and secure about her plans. When Becky told them that they should not worry, her father asked her how she felt when her cat disappeared for two days. "Worried," Becky replied. "Well," said her father. "That's how your mother and I feel when we don't know where you are."

As far as boys and cars were concerned, they said that as a 15-year-old ("Almost 16!" she interjected), they felt she was too young to be dating boys with cars. They would instead give her rides when needed, especially in the evening. But again, they emphasized, they wanted to know who these boys were, and most importantly to get to know the people with whom she would be spending time.

Nothing was accomplished overnight. It took months of talking, arguing, fighting—and more than a few icy family dinners. But the Simmonses could see that Becky's future was not beyond their reach. Becky was not like her older sister; she still (at that point) needed help to control her own destiny. Her parents' ability to say no gave Becky the opportunity to figure out her own values—and to be different from her sister, while still doing things that helped her feel good about herself.

MAINTAINING BOUNDARIES

We've mentioned several fads in general but have not focused in on any in depth. That's intentional; specific fads are relatively unimportant. Whether it's eating habits, speech, music, exercise, or technology—or some combination thereof—the subconscious motivation for any fad remains the same. Adolescents need to feel a sense of belonging; they must inhabit a world apart from our own (adult) world, and anything they can establish as routine—diet, talk, entertainment, health, computer use—has the potential to turn into a fad.

So in a way, even though a fad may appear to be haphazard—for instance, wearing mismatched sneakers—it is just another clear sign that adolescents are seeking some form of structure in their lives. Fads are simply attempts adolescents make at ordering, controlling, and finding outlets for their impulses. Peer groups support these attempts—just as they support the impulses—and parents need to recognize fads as adolescent experiments in seeking and using power to control their own lives.

Thus we must remember that adolescent fads *belong to adolescents*. They are not *our* fads; they are theirs. It is a grievous mistake for a parent to enter the adolescent world. When an adult tries to adopt the teenager's language, or to mimic dress or share in musical tastes, that parent is taking away something that belongs uniquely to the child, and the child's friends.

Although most adults do not completely resolve their adolescent issues, this does not mean that you must be a fully developed parent to be an effective POA. The trick is to keep your world separate from your child's. Tune in to the adolescent world *as it is,* not as you'd like it to be. Realize that your teenager's life is his or her own; stay away from it, especially if you see or sense that you are the only adult intruding on it. (If, for example, you look around and see that you are the only parent who shows up at every swim practice or play rehearsal, take a break.) Support your adolescents, but make sure you are not confusing their needs with your own.

Adolescents are enormously conscious of their parents, even if they don't always acknowledge their existence. They are acutely aware of how their parents look to themselves and, more importantly, to their friends. They don't want parents to look and act like teenagers, and parents shouldn't want to look or act like kids. It is imperative that parents honor the boundaries, in order that adolescents know what those boundaries are.

Dave could have been the poster boy for the prototypical adolescent. If you followed him with a camcorder, you would have used the tape for a study of the All-American 16-year-old.

School was as good as could reasonably be expected; he played sports well, was active in his community through a volunteer organization, and held a part-time job in the local pharmacy. He was well-known, well-liked, and respected.

Dave even got along fairly well with his parents. He knew the limits because they were clear, although he had his share of arguments attempting to get them altered. And he was able to argue well enough to bring about changes his parents felt were appropriate. Dave had a few close friends and a fair number of acquaintances. They were on the whole a "good bunch of kids," never getting in serious trouble although they sometimes had fun in ways not everyone approved of.

One of the activities that this group "invented" (they thought) was the scavenger hunt. Each week one teenager would devise a master list of items to scavenge for on Saturday night. The list would be copied; teams would be organized and off they would go—a dozen or two young people busy, talking, laughing, daring, "appropriating" some interesting items.

After a few of these hunts, word got around to parents. Dave's father, Joseph, was both pleased and interested. He liked the fact that his son was a leader in this activity and thought it great that the youngsters could come up with a clever, productive way to spend time. Joseph, being a clever man himself, thought his creativity and organizational skills could aid Dave and the hunt. He felt he could help make the lists, and that it might really turn into a "father and son" thing.

When Joseph approached Dave, telling him what he'd heard and how great he thought it was, Dave felt good. There was a certain amount of fear that his parents might not have liked the idea, what with kids racing all over town late at night, wasting gas—the usual parental complaints and "good reasons" not to do something fun. So Dave initially welcomed his father's input and assistance. Dave's house became the start and finish line on Saturday night, and Dave became the official judge.

Things went well the first time, but the second week three regulars failed to show up. By the next Saturday, several more players backed out. Dave felt uncomfortable because he knew his dad was particularly proud of that week's list. Dave also felt bad because he knew his father was trying to help, to be a "good guy," but things just weren't the same. And he felt distressed, too, because he didn't know how to say anything without hurting his father's feelings. He could see Joseph was having a lot of fun.

By the fifth week, the scavenger hunts were over. The fad had passed, and Dave never had to confront his father. The game had just died out; the players had drifted away. It was not until years later that Joseph learned that he had been responsible for the demise of the scavenger hunt.

Dave and his friends wanted time alone, needed the opportunity to be together and engage in an activity that was supervised by no one except themselves. To meet in a parking lot allowed them opportunities for spontaneity, freedom of expression, even socially unacceptable behavior—none of which they could do with Dave's dad there. These adolescents, like all teenagers, needed an outlet to express their own creativity and cleverness, not that of their parents. And although it was just a passing fad, they needed it to be all their own while it lasted.

However, with a little bit of tact parents can help youngsters find a resolution that enables them to have a strong sense of belonging to both a peer group and to their family while continuing to maintain a solid sense of who they are themselves. At the same time, parents can assuage some of their worry that their adolescent's faddish behavior will degenerate into a disastrous spiral to doom.

Take, for example, the often nettlesome question of proper attire for college interviews. Under seemingly impenetrable layers of obstinacy and outlandish dress, adolescents recognize that Something Big is happening when they talk to an admissions officer. They sense that this college stuff represents one of their first steps out into the adult world.

And yet ... they still need to be *told* that something is at stake here. They are so used to defending their style of dress against all adult importunities, that given the chance, many of them will stroll into a college interview sporting a concert t-shirt, surfer shorts, and sandals.

In this case, it is up to you to indicate what is and what is not appropriate garb. At times like this—when the situation requires it, and *when it is to their advantage*— adolescents know what standards apply, and most will be willing to follow them. They simply need—and want—a little pushing and prodding.

It is important to maintain the distinction between rebellion that takes place in a safe environment—home or school—and that occurring outside those relatively secure confines. If you ease off on the fads that are not destructive, if you save your emotional and oratorical firepower for faddish behavior that could instead prove to be self-destructive, then chances are much greater that you will find your adolescent ready to accept your advice on the issues you know (and he senses) really matter.

But no matter what you say, some youngsters will still show up for college interviews wearing Dayglo Mohawks. Let's assume your son is one who does. You must realize that it his *his* college acceptance—not yours—that may be in jeopardy, and you must act accordingly.

Maintain your composure as he walks out the door. No law says you must drive him there, if sitting in a college admissions waiting room while he looks like that will cause you undue stress. In your calmest voice, say something like: "I'm sorry you decided you have to keep your hair like that. It will be too bad if it works against you, and the school you really want to go to is put off by this. I hope for your sake it doesn't backfire."

If you can do that—if you can make your point calmly, clearly, and concisely—you will have taken a great stride toward crossing the peer pressure gulf that separates you from your adolescent, and avoiding a further confrontation over who is in charge. You will have shown him that this is not simply an us-against-them issue; you are not objecting to his peer group's look per se but rather you are reacting to a specific, situational issue. Just as importantly, you also will have indicated to him that he can be both part of his peer group *and* an appropriately clad college interviewee.

And speaking of peer pressure: Since you don't accept your son's argument, "Jojo gets to stay out to 2 A.M., so I should too," so neither should you accept his excuse, "That wasn't my wine in the car; I don't drink. I was just keeping it for Jojo." It's common for parents to hold an idealized view of their child's behavior, but too often that's an unrealistic view. If your adolescent lets his friends drink in his car—even if he himself doesn't—then isn't he part of a problem that must be addressed?

Try to avoid falling into the "my son's friends are a bad influence on him" trap. Your task is to focus on *your* adolescent and *his* development—not on anyone else's. Peer pressure and peer interaction is a tricky thing.

A GREAT BIG GAME

As a POA, you must be excruciatingly careful not to compete directly with your adolescent's peers. Rather, you must go around them—not circumvent them, exactly, but travel a circuitous path to prevent the fire of fads and friends from flaring into a major conflagration.

That's because, as you no doubt realize by now, "fads and friends" is really just a great big game. All adolescents are wizards at playing their peer group off against their parents. They know exactly how to use their friends to accomplish their immediate ends—the "but everyone else is doing it/you're the only parent who never ..." routine has been seared into the brains of all parents; we don't have to elaborate on it here.

But underneath the surface of that seemingly lopsided equation—"My friends are the most important thing in my life; my parents are pesky little gnats"—lies a much subtler dynamic. And it's one that you must learn to recognize so that you can place the "fads and friends" issue in the important context that it merits.

When adolescents haul out the heavy artillery—their friends, and the alleged hip actions of their ultra-cool parents—they are actually giving you a test. Do you really stand up for the values you claim to lay down, they are asking, or is this something they can talk you out of? Your response cannot be analyzed here—whether you do or do not change your mind about a certain action depends on the situation at hand, and on you and your family's values— but the point is simply stated: Sometimes "fads and friends" issues are not as clear-cut as they may seem.

Laura is the oldest of four children. Until her seventeenth birthday, she had been an exemplary girl. She went through junior high and the first three years of high school without incident. She was not terribly active socially, which had been a relief to her parents—especially when they heard stories from friends about the various crimes and misdemeanors of other adolescents.

Beginning with the birth of her brother when she was 3, Laura had been a second mother to her three siblings, enthusiastically keeping them clean, fed, and amused. Laura's parents found her to be an immense help and support. Up until the winter of her senior year, she had been the family's strongest advocate.

So it came as a surprise to them when she began to spend an extraordinary amount of time away from home. Even when she was home, she talked more on the telephone and less with her brothers and sisters. Her new cadre of friends resembled no one she had ever spent time with. Her taste in clothes grew more daring, at times resembling something out of the 1960s. Along with these changes came requests for freedom and demands to make her own decisions.

Her parents were able to see that Laura's adolescent rebellion was being compacted into the remaining time that she would spend in the fold of her family. At the end of the upcoming summer, she would be leaving home. But what concerned them most was that as a 17-year-old she might put herself in more dangerous positions than a 14-year-old would—and because she had avoided many of these "learning" situations at a younger age, they feared her judgment would not be good enough to avoid the pitfalls of adolescence. They knew that the next several months would be trying ones.

A string of countless arguments followed, mostly about being able to go places and about whom she would go there with. Concerts were okay on weekends, her parents decided, but they said no to an overnight trip to hear a group 300 miles away. They drew the line there, not because they didn't trust Laura but because they didn't feel she had enough experience saying no and was thus too vulnerable in that particular situation.

They spent hours listening to her thoughts and ideas about the world, knowing that she had much to learn; many of her ideas were sophomoric. But they also knew that if they listened to those ideas, they would be supporting her in developing her own way of thinking. To reject her thoughts at that point would only stop or impede her as she embarked on her new road toward independence.

Arguments about clothes centered only around the inappropriateness of a particular outfit. They knew she was developing a sense of sexuality and beginning to learn how to relate to young men. They realized she needed to experiment, but they knew that at 17 the demands would be greater than they would have been had she done her experimenting three years earlier. So they bit their tongues as a variety of unusual outfits appeared, saying "definitely not!" only to those that were blatantly revealing.

They withstood her arguments that "everyone dresses like this!" when they felt it was too provocative and would put Laura in a situation where she would have to deal with attitudes she had no experience with. At the same time they did allow her to explore her appearance and experience responses to it, including that of her first boyfriend.

It was difficult on the entire family. For the first time Laura—not anyone else—was receiving attention, and there was resistance and resentment. With three other children, jobs, obligations, and a constant blur of ongoing activities, it was a very difficult six months. But Laura's parents also knew this was the crucial beginning of their daughter's exploration of self. They had to be there to help her build a good foundation. Family values were the basic materials; Laura would have to find everything else she would need to construct the rest.

Sometimes adolescents are actually looking for an excuse for their parents to say no to them. When a teenager says, "I can't go with you guys. My dad would kill me if anybody ever saw the car parked there," he really means, "I'm scared to go there. My friends are trying to push me into a situation I don't want to be in. I need their approval, to provide strength in my search for my own identity, so I'll get it by pretending to want to go, while blaming not going on my parents." In addition to being "used" by your kids in situations that you're fully aware of ("All the other . . ."), you're also "used" by them at times you'll never even know about.

All of which means you must hone your listening skills to a razor-sharp edge, because from time to time your adolescent will bring to you a comment or request so unbelievably outrageous—so incredibly antithetical to every value you have ever held dear—that you must stop, take that by-now legendary step back, and examine exactly what he is saying. And when you do, you may very well find that he is asking you to say no.

Another example: Prom Night is near, and your daughter appears as you are studying some business reports, which she knows is the absolute worst time to talk to you. She opens the conversation with this spiel: "Dad, everybody's going to stay over at the hotel after the dance. Tommy and I want to get a room, too. Don't worry," she quickly adds, "we'll share it with Doug and Elyssa. So is it OK? And, um,

Tommy's kind of broke, and so am I, so can you help us pay for it?"

Something in her manner—the time she chose to approach you; her outlandish "request"; perhaps even her tone of voice—may tip you off that, despite her words asking you to say "Yes! Yes! Yes!" she actually is hoping you will say "No! No! No!"

Your interpretation of and subsequent reaction to her request depends, of course, upon your family's values, but if it is obviously something she is worried or ambivalent about, your course of action is clear. Just say, "I'm sorry, honey, but I'm really uncomfortable about this. I don't care whether you'll be staying alone with Tommy or with twenty other kids; this just doesn't suit our values. I'm sorry; the answer is no. End of discussion."

The actual argument may drag on a bit longer—primarily so that she can save face with her friends as she later retells this "battle" tale, than out of any great conviction on her part. In the end, by standing steadfast to your values, you will have performed a great service for your daughter. And it may be a service she did not even know she requested.

In situations such as this—when your son "wants" to host a party at your home while you're away ("I'm the only kid in school who hasn't had one all year"), or when your daughter "needs" to spend Friday night at the trendy new disco downtown ("I won't be popular anymore if you don't let me go")—you may see clearly that it's your adolescent who's being pressured by his or her friends, rather than you being pressured by your adolescent.

The teenage boy knows he would never be able to control his "guests" if you permitted him to have a party in your absence. Similarly, the teenage girl feels unsure of herself in a nightclub situation. Both adolescents are sending the same message; both are looking for parents to help them order their behavior, because they feel incapable of resisting the pressure and controlling it themselves.

Of course, that does not mean that these youngsters are ready and willing to lose face when you say "no." On the contrary, they are apt to return to their friends wearing hangdog faces, moaning "I hate my parents. I can't believe they won't let me (have a party) (go to Anthrax). They're so uncool!" Such complaints contribute to group belonging-ness, especially when everyone else in the group chimes in with, "Yeah, my parents too . . ."

From time to time, you may find yourself in a position to overhear such rabid antiparent talk. If you do, act deaf. Realize that it's not *you* they're talking about; it's simply their way of being valued members of the teenage tribe. Remember "fads and friends" is just a big, elaborate game.

Deafness and its companion, muteness, are extra-ordinary weapons, by the way. Nowhere is it written that you must react to or even acknowledge all adolescent fires. Nonresponses are perfectly legitimate. If you have said "no" and have nothing further to add—don't. Adolescent blazes burn out quickly unless you allow yourself to get drawn into them. In fact, you might even want to show your teen-agers that you can grunt—"Um hm. Yup. Hmm. Uh."—just as well as they do.

And if you absolutely, positively have to say something, make certain it is noncommittal: "I can see your point. I hear you. I'm sorry you feel that way." Don't repeat your previous "no"; simply terminate the discussion. Avoid being lured into a power struggle. You'll either lose it, or lose your mind trying to enforce whatever power you think you have.

Which brings us to the final point of this chapter: Never forget that "fads and friends" is a far trickier subject than it sounds, and it is a subject that many times will elude direct orders.

As a parent, you can legislate many things, but one thing you can absolutely not control is your adolescent's friends. You simply can't tell your son who he can or cannot see; you no longer have that dominance over his life. He enjoys too much independence and mobility for you to ever again say, "You cannot be friends with Elliot." You *can* say "Elliot cannot come over tonight," and you can even decree that he is not welcome at all, because this is an area in which your son's life interacts directly with your own. But you must know that your son will see Elliot sometime, somewhere.

And there will be many, similar areas of your adolescent's life you simply cannot control. So what should you do? Hold tight to your values; make sure they're solid and secure, and repeat them over and over again. The tighter you hold on, and the more you repeat them, the greater the chances that someday, somehow, your child will adopt them, too.

6 | **M**oods: The Teenager with a Thousand Faces

It's never easy to see your youngster fail a test, get cut from a sports team, or be rejected by a friend. His disappointment, embarrassment, or anger is expressed intensely, and he may be a bear to live with for awhile, particularly because while you watch, you hurt for him. But his emotions often stem from a clear, justifiable cause—one you may even be able to identify closely with—and you know from experience that his strong feelings will soon abate, and he will direct his energy elsewhere.

Mood swings, however, are entirely different. That loop-de-loop your adolescent rides between euphoria and sullenness, gregariousness and solitary confinement, is a peculiarly perplexing part of adolescence, especially because it is precipitated by unseen, unknown catalysts. Thus it becomes terribly difficult for parents and adolescents to deal with mood swings, simply because they seem to arrive with no known cause.

Any obscure, insignificant event—glimpsing two friends passing a note in class and being convinced he is the subject of that message, catching the end of a song on the radio—or even a non-event like not receiving a phone call can plunge teenagers into an abyss of despair or send them soaring into flights of elation. The catch is that you as a parent have no clue as to the meaning behind these split-second shifts of mood.

Research has shown that adolescent mood swings are *not*, in fact, wilder or more abrupt than those that occur during other phases of life. What makes adolescent mood swings so remarkable and worrisome to parents, however, is that the behavior that accompanies them is so radically different from the way the youngster acted before charging full tilt into adolescence. Adolescents have not yet learned to mask their feelings.

For the first time in his life, an adolescent is able to follow up his actions—physically and emotionally—in dangerous ways. It's one thing for an infant to toss a bottle, or for a 7-year-old to kick and scream. They're unpleasant sights, but they cannot approach the gruesomeness of watching a teenage boy slam his fist into a wall or race his car out of the driveway in a rage, or having a teenage girl not come home for several days and nights.

Virtually all adolescents experience unexplained mood swings. Your son may come home from swim practice full of animation, then appear for dinner forty-five minutes later looking as if he alone bears the burden of saving the world.

Suddenly the phone rings, and once again he becomes the epitome of charm and good will. What happened in those intervening moments? Did anything change? What have you missed?

Even the most observant parental eye cannot discern the precipitating factors for such behavior. It *is* bewildering, but that does not imply such behavior is random. It truly does have meaning, although you will sometimes need the detective skills of Sherlock Holmes to figure out what that meaning is. The most innocuous remark—"Do you mind setting the table tonight?"—can trigger waves of helplessness in an adolescent. "Why does everybody treat me like a kid! How come I never have any power in this house! When will I ever get to boss people around!" might be the feelings caroming through his subconscious. Meanwhile, all he does is slam the dishes onto the counter in an awesome display of rage. Stunned onlookers have no clue as to why he is acting this way—and neither does he.

If he could verbalize his feelings, he might say, "I'm searching for my own identity. I'm feeling ambivalent about many things, and I'm vulnerable to many outside forces. I wish I could speak these words, but I don't even recognize that I'm having these thoughts."

Kate was experiencing such feelings, although she seemed to be getting through her adolescent years with a minimum of outward fuss. Her friends phoned often, and she was a constant jewel in her parents' busy lives. Her oldest sister, Kerry, who was her mentor and best friend, had departed in September for a well-known college, following a very successful high school career. Kate seemed to be comfortable in her junior year at that same school, maintaining good grades and being genuinely involved in a few positive extracurricular activities.

Now, with their focus on a single child at home, her parents often spent dinner talking about how happy Kerry seemed to be at her prestigious university, and how wonderful it was that she had been so successful in high school that she'd been able to get in there. They often mentioned how much they missed Kerry, and how much they would miss Kate when she went off to the university in just two short years. A sticker from Kerry's college was plastered on the rear windows of both cars, and every member of the family had clothes from the college bookstore for every possible occasion.

Halfway through her junior year, Kate stopped going to the nursing home where she had volunteered for the previous year and a half (she "adopted" two grandparents twice a week). She dropped down one level in English, explaining the higher track course took too much time, and her math class became a battleground, even though she had done so well with the same teacher the year before. She burst into tears over trivial-seeming matters, and behaved more like the Shakespearean character who was her namesake rather than the young woman her parents thought they knew so well.

Her mother finally got a clue when asking an innocent, parental-type question: "How'd the functions test go today?" This brought forth a stinging adolescent-type answer: "How come you keep asking me that? I just want to forget about school and all the pressure my teachers and you guys put on me. I know I didn't study hard enough because I was worried about the fight Patti and I had, but you don't have to keep reminding me . . . and . . . and . . . maybe because I don't do as well in school I won't get into as good a college as Kerry did . . ."

Up to that moment Kate had not been able to articulate her thoughts, and so the outside world had seen a happy-go-lucky girl suddenly transformed into a tigress capable only of snarling "Why don't you just shut up?" in several different forms. Thus the myth of adolescent mood swings as an arcane, inexplicable phenomenon was reinforced once more, erroneously. But mood swings often have very rational, quite understandable roots.

The parent's task is to remember that, no matter how sharp or bizarre the mood swing is, all behavior has meaning. For instance, if your question "Do you want to go to the movies with us Friday night?" unleashes a flood of teenage tears, it may be because the two words "Friday night" bring up images of a party she fears she won't be invited to. The adolescent brain is capable of twisting this further to mean, "Even my parents are torturing me by reminding me I'm a social zero."

Victor and Donny had been best friends since sixth grade. They had survived the often traumatic junior high years, maintaining unswerving loyalty to one another and to their friendship. They had both made the high school freshman football team, were holding their own in the considerably larger high school setting, and continued to spend most weekends zooming in and out of each other's homes, engaged in a wide variety of activities.

In January of that freshman year Donny's parents noticed that a strange quiet had descended over the household. Their son came straight home from school, went into his room, and closed the door. Gentle questions about what was happening in his life brought forth sullen or inane nonanswers; more persistent inquiries elicited even less. Donny began hanging around the house all weekend long, and Victor's calls and appearances became infrequent.

Donny's parents asked Victor's parents if they had noticed any differences in Victor's behavior. They were told that his social world was widening. Victor went to parties nearly every weekend. They also told Donny's parents that although both of them worked and did not get home until after six o'clock, they noticed that the house always looked as if a number of teenagers had been "making themselves comfortable."

That spring the only change in Donny was an increase in the volume of music enveloping his room, and increasingly monosyllabic responses to any words addressed his way. Then in late May the local paper reported the arrest of twelve freshman boys for possession of a keg of beer; one of the names was Victor's. When Donny's parents asked him what he knew, he smashed one fist into another and yelled, "I told him those guys were stupid. He's been drinking and partying with them all year, ever since football ended. They do stuff every afternoon. I didn't know what else to do. Victor doesn't like me anymore."

No parent in the world can know everything that goes on between school walls, in a friend's car, or even over one's own telephone lines. No human being can reconstruct the thought process that turns a lovable adolescent into Count Dracula, then back into Mother Teresa, all in the space of one weekend morning.

So how do you live with it?

One way is not to take adolescent moods or mood swings personally. They are not directed at you as a parent, so you should not turn them into parent-child confrontations. Far better to accept mood swings and live with them as a natural phase of adolescence, than to man the barricades and prepare for trench warfare every time Little Miss Personality metamorphoses into Captain Miserable. Escalation is no way to win this battle.

Of course, this advice is easier to give than to follow. We are not saying that you should allow asocial behavior to permeate, even control, your home, but mild behavior can occasionally be overlooked; it probably will be outgrown relatively quickly. In the short run this may seem like surrender, but in the long run it may be the wisest course of action to take.

Acknowledging mood-swinging behavior can also be helpful. Say, "Lauren, it's okay for you to be mad or cranky." Then pause and say, "But in this house it's not okay to be rude, or to inflict your bad mood on the whole family. I'm sorry you're so upset (pause again). Dinner's in half an hour and I'll see you then," means you've acknowledged your adolescent's feelings—and you've also absorbed some of them. Perhaps she no longer feels alone, now that she hears you're not mad that she's mad; maybe she sees your point of view and returns to her room determined to use the next thirty minutes to work herself out of her black mood, before coming to dinner feeling more comfortable with her world—and yours.

Then again, maybe she doesn't. She very well may show up for dinner glowering like Ty Cobb, emanating "come near me and I'll kill you" vibes from every pore of her body. In such a situation, the question becomes should you force her to sit at the table and act like a civilized human being, or is it wiser to suggest she excuse herself to spare the rest of the family from the onslaught of her agonies?

It depends. One family's values might hold that when everyone is home, everyone eats together; in another family, peace and harmony might take priority over eating dinner together. Your decision to demand her presence, or let her banish herself, is yours alone to make. Whatever you decide, it must be based on your own family values, and it must be consistent with everything you've decided before. Consistency is crucial. As a POA, you must be the stable voice of consistency, amidst the turmoil of your adolescent's inconsistent mood swings.

FINDING THE COURAGE TO SAY NO

While we believe it is important for parents to be able to say no to their adolescents, we also believe that parents must find the courage to say no to their own impulses to demand certain behavior from their adolescents. In other words, when dealing with mood swings parents need the courage to say no to their own impulse to say no. Got that?

Here's what we mean. A natural instinct when faced with precipitous mood swings is to lash out and demand conformity to "acceptable" standards of behavior. But that impulse is driven largely by frustration, and it must be stifled in order to steady the mood-swinging pendulum. Despite the difficulty mood swings create for an entire family, they are seldom behaviors that adolescents can control, let alone understand, and parents must realize that mood swings, by their transitory nature, are better tolerated than confronted angrily.

Fight the impulse to say no when the mood is swinging upward too. When your son is wildly euphoric—a couple of older boys have just asked him to play guitar in their band, and he's already begun planning next year's North American tour—try to resist the impulse to haul him back down to earth with reminders of school commitments, the cutthroat nature of the music industry, and his own fairly limited musical ability.

You need not encourage his unrealistic fantasies, of course, but a realistic, neutral response ("This must be one of the most exciting days of your life!") that recognizes and acknowledges his feelings, while not feeding them, can go a long way toward avoiding hurt, anger or misunderstanding on the day the dream turns sour.

Of course, saying no to your own impulses is not easy when dealing with mood swings because the meaning behind such behavior is seldom discernible. Although you may be unable to find clear, understandable causes, you still can make the assumption that *something* has occurred that threatens your adolescent's burgeoning sense of identity or self-esteem. No mood is unprecipitated—though the precipitating factor may be unknown to both parent and adolescent. So even if you are unaware that an English teacher made a searing remark about students who are unprepared, or the seating pattern on the school bus has suddenly yet subtly shifted, or the bathroom scale registered a quarter-pound leap, you can still empathize with your mood-swinging adolescent.

Empathy requires that you think about how *you* feel when *your* self-esteem is threatened, when you receive a terse note from your boss asking to see her as soon as possible, for instance, or when someone cracks a cocktail party joke about people with thinning hair. Threats to self-esteem are not limited to the adolescent world, but adolescent defense systems are not nearly as developed as those of adults, so teenagers will naturally react more sharply than adults do to such threats. That is an unfortunate fact of life for those of us who must share homes with them, but it is as much a burden of adolescence as of parenthood. And remember, adolescents don't enjoy their mood swings any more than we do.

ACKNOWLEDGING FEELINGS

Occasionally, of course, adolescents may volunteer information as to why they feel the way they do. When this happens, try not to minimize it. Much as you'd love to say it, "You're all upset because she said *that?*" is not the proper response to "Mom, Mindy says my haircut looks like a dog's." While your intention might be admirable—to make your daughter feel good by using your wisdom to reveal that what she perceives to be a major problem is, in fact, an itty-bitty triviality—your words will not come across as helpful or comforting. They'll sound trivializing, and that will only feed her sense of despair.

Aim instead for one of those neutral responses: "That must've really upset you, huh? You must not have expected Mindy to say that at all." By saying this, you have avoided both taking sides and minimizing the issue (no matter how much you agree with Mindy, or how inane the issue has become), while you have legitimized your daughter's feelings, and in doing so have also helped her feel less lonely.

Many parents today do everything they can to make sure their children experience no anxiety or depression. From the day they gave birth to their children, they have smoothed their road of any bumps, potholes, or even curves, but no such highway to adulthood exists. As a result, when anxiety or depression does occur, it is seen as an unnatural or fearful emotion. The adolescent feels ill-equipped to deal with it, and so the emotions return even stronger, each successive wave growing higher and more threatening.

Todd was a golden child. He was bright, athletic and well-liked by all. Teachers sang his praises; friends called constantly; he was a joy to live with. He knew the right words for every situation, and could make whoever was around him feel good. If he set a goal, he attained it. He was never disappointed, and he never disappointed anyone.

One day Todd tried out for the male lead in the high school musical. He didn't get it, although he did make the chorus. The afternoon that the cast was announced he stormed into the house, slammed the door, and locked himself in his room. His mother knocked once, then knocked again. There was no reply.

She knew that something was awry, and the temptation to call out was strong. She raised her hand to knock again, then pulled it down, biting back the "Todd, is there anything wrong?" question rising to the tip of her tongue. She went downstairs and considered calling the head of the drama group to find out what was going on, but as she finished dialing she hung up quickly, and went to the kitchen to prepare dinner.

An hour later, she met her husband at the door. She kissed him hello, and he immediately asked, "What's the matter?"

"I have a feeling Todd didn't get the part. He locked himself in his room. I think we better give him some time," she replied.

As Todd's father passed the closed door he called out, "Hey, Todd." When there was no response he, too, left him alone.

An hour after that Todd's mother called up to let him know dinner was ready. Todd came down; the first thing he said was, "I didn't get the lead. Jono did. He deserved it. But I made the chorus."

The crisis had passed. With no interference Todd had worked through his anger and disappointment, and felt ready to cope with his world again.

Parents must feel confident when their adolescent's mood turns grim and feel equally comfortable in letting their teenager confront those moods, largely by themselves—just as it is important for parents to do the same thing with their own moods.

Escaping bad moods is just as unnatural a defense mechanism as denying that they exist; it's simply another form of escalation. The parent who says, "Oh, I can see you're feeling bad. Let's go shopping; that'll take your mind off things!" does not send a message of hope, does not help her adolescent learn how to deal with her burgeoning senses of identity and self-esteem. Rather, she sends a message that neither the parent nor the adolescent can deal with worry or fear, so they must pretend their emotions do not exist. But, of course, they do, and parents who do not teach their adolescents how to deal with minor worries and fears when they are young will never equip them with the tools to handle life's bigger problems. We are all disappointed some of the time.

KEEPING YOUR FEELINGS SEPARATE

Adolescents have an inherent talent for making extraordinary issues out of the most ordinary things; mood changes occur with stunning regularity, and they can be contagious. Adolescent mood swings can infect parents in a moment, and before anyone knows why, an entire household is infested with anxiety or anger, euphoria or hilarity.

Some parents allow their moods to mirror their children's, and that gives adolescents an enormous if often unrecognized source of power. A tired mother picks up her daughter at school, and the girl's ebullience lifts her mother's flagging spirits. Then, for some indeterminate reason—perhaps a glimpse of a friend riding in a car with a boy, or the sudden memory of a lunchroom slight?—the girl's mood sinks. It takes awhile for the mother to realize this, but in time she picks up on the new "down" mood, and again reflects it. The mother is left feeling lost and concerned, when with little fanfare her daughter has already begun to rebound.

An effective parent must remember to separate her adolescent's feelings from her own. She cannot attribute her own teenage memories to her adolescent. Only by maintaining her own identity can she help her teenager develop her own sense of self. It is only when parents are able to order their own responses to adolescent moods that they can develop the kind of communication that will bring into the open the catalysts that drive these mood swings, and keep those swings from seriously affecting every member of the family. The more parents can help adolescents order their own behavior by being clear, consistent, and value-oriented in their own actions, the more comfortable and less combative the entire family will become.

And that, in turn, will make it far easier to deal with the more dangerous issues of adolescence, such as drugs, alcohol, and sexuality.

7 | Sexuality: The Mating Game

The boy and girl are only 14 years old, but they claim to be as much in love as any adults. Although their parents disapprove of the relationship and forbid the couple from ever dating again, they sneak away and meet. But tragedy strikes—they choose to kill themselves, rather than live without each other. Whenever this story is told, people get all caught up, for teenage love never fails to generate intense feelings in adults as they remember first crushes and sexual urges.

The tragic couple was, of course, Romeo and Juliet but it could be any teenagers, for impulsive teenage sexual behavior has been common to all eras. And for hundreds of years, from Shakespearean drama to Broadway, from *West*

Side Story to *The Blue Lagoon*, adults have viewed sexual feelings between teenagers as natural, lovely, and exciting.

But at the same time we romanticize adolescent sexuality and actively support it—by making encouraging remarks, lending clothing and cars for dates, even providing birth control devices. Yet we are intimidated by it. We don't want our youngsters to "go all the way," and we don't want to hear about it when they do. We become apprehensive when girlfriend retreats into boyfriend's room and shuts the door. We experience mixed emotions when our son wears skin-tight Lycra biking shorts (never mind that his last bike trip occurred when he was nine), or our daughter drives off to school sporting a tank top that leaves precious little to anyone's imagination.

Parents have always had muddled feelings about teens and sex, but in the '90s they have more reasons than in past decades to feel pushed in one direction, then pulled in another. Most parents of today's adolescents were children during the '50s and teenagers in the '60s. When they were youngsters, the grandfatherly Eisenhowers inhabited the White House, and Beaver Cleaver lived in Mayfield. In their teenage years, the glamorous Kennedys took over Washington, and Eldridge Cleaver was all over the tube. Then our leaders were gunned down, our country went to war, and for a number of years the only way to feel good was to act out a range of impulses, including sexual ones.

Those who learned about sexuality in the rigid '50s reached sexual maturity (biologically speaking, at least) in the '60s, when the operative phrase was far from subtle: "Make love, not war." Being labeled "the love generation" provided a great excuse for a tidal wave of promiscuity, and even if everyone did not *participate* in the sexual revolution, everyone was exposed to it.

That raises a conundrum: the same parents who as adolescents were affected by the sexual revolution are now parents of adolescents who take the changes wrought by that revolution for granted, and many times it is difficult to face the new sexual landscape from the other side of the generational fence.

Throughout this book, we have not tried to impose our own values on others; however, we feel we must say that the sexual revolution has caused a great deal of harm for adolescents. It has given them permission to act on their biological urges, not postpone them until they are emotionally ready to deal with them. They are unable in many ways to cope with the images and ideas that surround them, in movies, magazines, music, and television. This unfortunate change in cultural values has left many adolescents feeling lost, confused, and under a great deal of pressure.

That is why you must be certain your teenager has a good sexual education—and that doesn't mean simply attending a class in school. There is no area more crucial for the discussion of family values than sexuality. Given the prevalence of sexual imagery all around us, it is imperative that parents give their children facts about sex—*within their own family values systems*, of course. And it is imperative that parents examine their own value systems, so that the information that is conveyed through discussions and conversations includes not only facts about physical acts, but involves the emotional component of sex as well.

Sexual education is not an issue that can be left to peers, or schools, or television. You will find, however, that this is the area your adolescent will be most reluctant to discuss openly with you; sharing concerns, even thoughts, about sexuality does not come easily for anyone, especially a teenager who is stumbling upon the subject for the very first time.

So parents must work hard to draw their adolescents out. You must strive to talk openly—about the emotional component of a sexual relationship; about safe sex; about the consequences of acting on impulses, and about the consequences of a teenage pregnancy.

If parents set forth family values, their teenagers will have the sense that there is a support system available; they will know that the decisions they make will not have to be theirs alone.

We've said over and over in this book that you should try to avoid responding precipitously to your adolescent's statements and actions; instead, identify your own values, and talk about them. That is certainly true with issues of sexuality. When you find out your daughter is sexually active, you need to be able to avoid one of two reflexive reactions (either rushing out to the gynecologist to fit her for a diaphragm, or screaming, "How could you do this to me?"). It's not an easy thing to do, but you must let her know that your door is always open for discussion. Even if she doesn't feel comfortable, at the moment, peeking through it.

Sexuality in the '50s was more talk than action; then through the decades of the '60s, '70s, and '80s the pendulum swung dramatically in the other direction. There are signs that the pendulum of sexual mores is swinging back again in the '90s. The twin specters of herpes and AIDS have demonstrated chillingly that too much of anything *can* be bad—can be deadly, in fact. The heady "we can change the world" optimism of the '60s has given way to a feeling of helplessness, as environmental and social problems rain down upon us and our children. Sexual behavior has always been tied to political, economic and social trends, but perhaps never in history have those trends been more uncertain. "Lifestyles of the Rich and Famous" appears on television, while more than a million Americans live on streets. We see near-pornographic ads in magazines, yet turn the page to read a public service message about sexually transmitted diseases. We want our children to be attractive, popular, and desirable to the opposite sex, but we don't want them to be libertines.

Although our society is more open sexually and aware, teenagers are becoming more sexually cautious and discreet. What is different about their behavior is that they feel more sexually entitled, and they are not ashamed or fearful of their emerging feelings. Perhaps this will enable our adolescents to enter the world of sexuality with a stronger sense of their needs, and a more optimistic sense that those needs are natural and will be fulfilled in the course of time. Delay of gratification does not mean that the eventual outcome will not be positive. It is our view that some delay of sexual gratification may even enhance the outcome.

An issue as explosive, dangerous, and mysterious as sexuality is one that demands particularly strong and consistent parental leadership. Unfortunately, it is also an issue about which parents are often concerned, confused, and inconsistent.

The first step toward clarity is to realize that sexual behavior, like all other adolescent behavior, has meaning. When teenagers act upon their sexual feelings—and this could mean anything from masturbation to intercourse, from asking you about your own sexual history to telling you about their latest exploits—they are adolescents testing limits. And they are testing two limits simultaneously: yours, to see whether you are really in charge of the family, and theirs, to determine if they have the ability to control their own impulses. Sexuality cascades down upon the adolescent, both in feelings toward the same sex and the opposite sex. These feelings are important parts of a growing sense of sexual self.

A teenager's sense of sexuality stems from many sources. Parents are major influences. Children pick up cues quite early in life from such things as how comfortable Mommy and Daddy are with their own sexuality, and how affectionate they are with each other—but there are other factors. Society influences sexuality, through everything from rock lyrics to newspaper headlines; so do such moments as unexpectedly catching a glimpse of your body in a full-length mirror.

Yet it's very difficult for parents to know or acknowledge, let alone control, most of these influences. It's tough to understand what effect AIDS "jokes" have on an adolescent's sexual feelings or behavior, just as it's nearly impossible to monitor the amount or type of information (or misinformation) your teen is receiving in the locker room, at the diner, or from co-workers at the supermarket. These are facts of life (so to speak) over which parents have little control, and it is naturally very frustrating.

But parents *can* control their own words and deeds, *can* moderate their own tones of voice and their actions, and thus *can* influence their adolescent's struggle to develop both a sexual identity and an acceptable standard of sexual behavior. And perhaps more than in any other area of parenthood, a prior understanding of your own sexual values, as well as a consistent manner of applying those values, is crucial.

You must feel comfortable communicating family values about sexuality to your adolescent, and your must continue to convey them, even in the face of heated opposition. If you do not feel at ease having your daughter go away for a weekend with her boyfriend's family; if you get nervous thinking of your son entertaining his girlfriend in your finished basement; if you do not wish to view a poster of a man's bare buttocks every time you walk into your daughter's room—then let your child know it. Show by what you say, what you do, even how you dress, that there are certain types of acceptable sexual behaviors in your home, and certain behaviors that are unacceptable. Be consistent when you show your adolescents which is which. Inconsistency can be dangerous. Your concern about the sexual messages you are sending to your daughter can be perplexing—as they were to Edie.

Edie, 16, had never been the life of the party. She had avoided boys ever since middle school, always preferring the companionship of girls. Attractive, almost exotic, everyone knew her time would come; however, it was painful to her parents to see her not go out, and instead sit at home every New Year's Eve, or earn money babysitting long after her contemporaries had ceased to be available.

When Peter became interested in her, it was as if a sudden glow had permeated their home. Edie's demeanor and outlook brightened; she became a pleasure to be around. The relationship began with gusto, and picked up from there. There were incessant phone calls, after school study sessions, even shared rides to school every morning. It was young love in its purest and most robust form.

Yet a rule had been established in Edie's home: "No boys in your room unless the door is open."

What should her parents do? Should they change the rule, and permit Peter and Edie to spend time in her room alone? It would be easy to turn their heads, because the change

Peter had wrought in Edie was so wonderful—but that would have blurred the boundary lines of appropriate sexual behavior. In addition, it would have made it more difficult for Edie to determine whether her parents were still in charge of her, and whether she was in control of her own feelings.

We are suggesting that the rules and codes of the house be stated simply and clearly, and enforced consistently. When Edie's parents said, "In this house, no room except ours—the parents'—has closed doors when someone of the opposite sex is inside," they were setting forth their values in a clear and helpful manner. They were not being inconsistent, nor were they saying that the two adolescents did not have a valid relationship. What they were saying was that in their home, adolescents must be aware of rules and boundaries—no ifs, ands or "but MOMs" about it.

Similarly, if you have always taught your children that the human body is a wonderful thing and should be treated with respect, yet you persist in parading around in front of your 13-year-old clothed only in your underwear, you send a mixed message. For years your family may have been comfortable with their bodies; no one felt embarrassed or self-conscious about their natural functions. It seemed prudish, even absurd, to cover up when things were so natural.

Yet you must recognize that when puberty strikes, times change. The home becomes a very different place when an adolescent takes up residence. Adolescents are easily aroused—that's normal and good—so parents must take responsibility for not placing them in situations where they will become unduly aroused. You must be careful not to confuse openness with provocation.

And if you are a parent who adheres to a "double stan-dard," say by permitting a son to have a later curfew than a daughter of the same age, then you may want to spend some time checking your own values for consistency. You probably need to better ensure that the messages you send your adolescent are clear, concise, and consistent.

Double standards occur often, and without thinking. The real problem with double standards for males and females is that all family members will know about them, there being few secrets in any family. If your daughter recognizes a set of standards for her brother that are not the same as hers, then she will be—rightfully—indignant.

Perhaps you were raised to believe that double stan-dards are not only appropriate, but necessary. Well, times have changed. You must be aware that women do not relish the sexual shackles that tradition has placed on them—even your daughters. Ask them about their feelings; it is a terrific opportunity to hear how the young women of the '90s see their place in the future. Then the messages that you send to them will have a meaning and purpose that is both important and educational.

Jake's parents knew that their son, age 14, was becoming interested in girls. Showers no longer had to be requested (or demanded); clothes ceased to be selected randomly. Phone calls from girls no longer concerned missed homework assignments, and parties began to fill his social calendar.

When Steffi became his "girlfriend," Jake's parents felt that he had entered into a new phase of life. Although slightly embarrassed, his father felt almost prideful when he found a packet of condoms in Jake's wallet. Yet he had reacted with hurt and anger toward Barbara, Jake's older sister, two years earlier when he had discovered the same type of birth control device in her backpack. Barbara had also undergone a social transformation, and had entered into a more sociable group of friends.

Both acts represented a statement about sexual experiences —perhaps a plan, perhaps a boast, in many cases a hope. Parental reactions to these inevitable events are crucial to their youngsters' sensitivities. When you make the type of discoveries that Jake and Barbara's father did, you can react with pride, or anger—or you can seize it as an excellent opportunity for open discussion, and a rechecking and understanding of your own values.

Here's another example of inconsistent behavior, from a single-parent family. (The upsurge of divorce and separation has created ambiguities never before seen in American society. There are no hard and fast rules regarding protocol in such situations—but if ever there was a time to hold onto a secure value system, it is now.)

Liz is 15; she lives with her mother during the week, but spends nearly every weekend at her father's apartment. Her parents' divorce has been final for only two months, but already her mother's new boyfriend has moved into the house, and her father "entertains" a certain woman every weekend that Liz is there.

One tumultuous Sunday, Liz asks both parents: "If you can sleep with someone without being married, why can't I?"

The answer is both simple and complex. The simple response is, "Because we're adults, and you're not. Just because you and I are both single doesn't mean we're the same."

The complex response demands that both parents examine their own sexual behavior. They must check their own values, motives, and actions, and determine whether they've moved too quickly into a new live-in relationship. Divorce is a tough situation for children of *any* age to deal with; adolescents find it particularly difficult, because it stirs up questions of sexuality at the very time their own sexual stewpot is bubbling over. When parents then begin exhibiting adolescent sexual behavior themselves—that is, dating, "going steady," or "sleeping around"—their youngsters' confusion can be overwhelming indeed.

But being sensitive to your adolescents' sexual sensibilities does not mean you must stow your own libido in the deep freeze. When a marriage breaks up, you have every right to pursue a new social life. Just take care to do it gradually, responsibly, and caringly.

Because sex can be used as a weapon—by parents as well as adolescents, the user may not even realize what he or she is doing.

Take the case of Claudette and her 14-year-old son Marc. For years, it was a Sunday morning tradition for the family to sprawl all over the double bed in the master bedroom, reading the paper, and munching muffins. When Marc's father moved out, the dynamics changed. Marc may have spent nearly every Sunday morning of his life lounging in that comfortable bed, but the meaning of that behavior changed, and grew vastly more complicated, the moment his same-sex parent was not there to protect Marc from his very natural impulses and fantasies.

Claudette must remember the danger of impulsiveness that threatens all youngsters. She needs to make sacrifices, to observe strict boundaries, so that her son's fantasies will not have free rein. In this instance, the courage to say no means the courage to reformulate existing boundaries, even if it involves something as innocuous, and tradition-bound, as reading the Sunday newspaper together in bed.

Keep in mind that we are not suggesting that parents no longer cuddle with or embrace their children. To hold an adolescent at arm's length can suggest rejection. What we are suggesting is that the complexities of sexual feelings are different within cultures and within families, and to be aware of the messages of your actions toward your teenagers.

As in many other areas of adolescence, our youngsters' comments about, and actions involving, sexual behavior indicate that they do not want to be given a free hand to follow every single urge that courses through their bodies. Rather, they are seeking input to establish guidelines for their behavior. Your job as parents is to pass your values along to your teenagers.

This is not always easy to do, however. While you may know deep down you you feel, and what you would like to say to your teenagers—"Sexual feelings are normal and healthy; it is exciting to learn that people are attracted to you; we want you to be comfortable with your feelings, but also want to help you avoid acting in ways that could hurt you"—you may not always be able to express those thoughts. Many times, our actions belie our best intentions.

Take the case of Robin, a 15-year-old whose reward for good grades was a trip to the cosmetics counter at the local mall, where she was encouraged to try on makeup, have her colors analyzed and buy, in her mother's words, "a sexy outfit that really shows off your body." Without meaning to, Robin's mother sent her a contradictory message that what counts in life is *not* intellectual prowess and academic achievement, but rather good looks and great legs.

It works the same with sons, of course. Ryan's father passes on his attitude that unfamiliar women may be treated as objects when he hands over the binoculars to his son in a crowded stadium and tells him to "check out the one in Section 23. How about *that* set?!" That is a different type of contradictory message. In this seemingly innocuous, "manly" message, Dad has conveyed an important set of values. He is saying that the game is less important than some transient sexual fantasy he encounters. In sharing this fantasy with his son, he is minimizing their relationship, degrading women, and transmitting a set of values that upon reflection may even prove embarrassing.

Chaz's parents are delighted that, at 17, he has finally found a girlfriend. Marissa is all they had hoped for in a first girlfriend: appropriately giddy, goal directed, perhaps even the teenage daughter they longed to have themselves. In the three months they have been going out, Chaz's grades have gone up, as has the amount of time he spends brushing his teeth. Chaz's parents are falling in love with Marissa.

It is always easier to be parental and accepting of a child who is not one's own; one unusual aspect of parenting an adolescent is that it is often more comfortable to be understanding of your child's same sex friend, or even of a boyfriend or girlfriend, than with your own offspring. Expectations and hopes cloud our view of our own children; these blocks do not exist with other youngsters, and we find ourselves more gracious and understanding of behavior that we would not have permitted within our own families. So it was with Marissa and Chaz.

If Marissa stayed out late, there was always an excuse that was acceptable and plausible. Chaz's parents began to value Marissa more than their son. They attended her dance recitals, found themselves clothes shopping for her, and when they traveled they would bring gifts for her as well as for him. When they sent away for theater tickets, they were certain to include Chaz and Marissa in their plans.

But now problems have suddenly arisen. When Chaz begins to stay out all night, his parents hesitate to say anything; after encouraging an "adult" relationship, they have surrendered their ability to say no to, and place limits on, their adolescent.

Chaz, too, feels awkward; he is overwhelmed by the feeling of going out at night with his parents *and* his girlfriend. He senses he is being forced into an adult relationship with Marissa sooner than he is ready, and instead of saying "No! No! No!," as he expects and wants his parents to, their actions are telling him "Yes! Yes! Yes!"

Chaz's parents have, in their blurring of their own needs and desires, robbed him of an important aspect of being a teenager: The ability to experiment with many friends, in different ways and in different settings. His parents had locked him prematurely in a relationship that he was not prepared to sustain forever.

The pace of the adolescent sexual metronome should be set by the adolescent, not the parent, within appropriate limits and boundaries. Meanwhile, the parents' role is to support that metronome, by making sure that it is not running too fast for the adolescent. If the parents are secure in their own sexuality and values; if they show (by their words and deeds) that sex is emotional as well as physical; warm as well as hot; a commitment as well as an act, then they will have less difficulty monitoring that metronome than if they send mixed messages, set double standards, or are uncertain of their own sexual values.

In sexuality, more than in perhaps any other area of parenthood, parents must make the decision to communicate with their teenagers openly and sensitively—even if, at times, the communication seems to take place in only one direction. For instance, this can happen when a parent who has always conveyed disapproval of premarital sex receives clear signals (say, birth control devices left "mistakenly" on the bed) that the adolescent is engaged in exactly that.

Though the initial reaction might be that any further discussion is futile, that's not the case. The teenager might be sending the signal that sex is confusing or pressure-filled or anxiety-provoking; the signal might actually say, "I need to talk." Just because an adolescent has taken matters of sexuality into his or her own hands doesn't mean that the course is irreversible. An adolescent is still a teenager, still needs guidance. The job of a parent is to show the teenager that, while his or her actions may have been impulsive, there still are options available. And those options are best communicated through clear, open discussion. Or by writing.

Mel, a conscientious and caring parent, has become deeply concerned when he learns that AIDS is making inroads on college campuses. His son Curtis is a freshman, away from home for the first time. In one of his weekly letters Mel cautions him—gently—about the dangers of sexual experimentation.

"Be careful," he writes. "That cute girl you think has a background just like yours may have made one bad choice a couple of years ago. Perhaps several years ago, just when she was coming into her own feelings of sexuality and rebellion, she began flirting with a tattooed muscular young man who worked as a landscaper near her home. (You never know!) He might have driven a large and impressive motorcycle, and when he asked her to take a ride it was as if a knight on a white charger had come into her life. An occasional intravenous drug user, the young man had used the wrong needle several years ago and was now a carrier for HIV. For our adorable coed, this relationship became her first sexual encounter, a relationship that was fleeting but very, very contagious."

Mel was surprised—and hurt—when Curtis wrote a very brief note in return: "Thanks for the advice, Dad, but I can take care of myself."

Several weeks later Mel found himself nearby on business, so as a surprise he knocked on Curtis' door. Imagine *Mel's* surprise when he saw on Curtis' mirror—taped among various photographs and ticket stubs—his letter. Highlighted in yellow was Mel's warning on AIDS.

There is an important moral in this little tale: Have faith that what you want to say is right. Send your message, or state your case, even if you're not sure it's being received or heard. No parent can control the receiver of a message—but neither can any parent abrogate the responsibility to send it. Where adolescents are concerned, the feedback may not be immediate—but, rest assured, the payoff will eventually come.

Sending the correct sexual messages is not an easy task. There is, unfortunately, no guide out of this maze. But often the struggle results in rewards such as the one Mel received. Those kinds of rewards are not always forthcoming, or even expressed, but they are acted out in positive behavior patterns.

Ruth decided that her new boyfriend would be Jesse—a choice that made her parents cringe. He was everything they would not want for their daughter: unkempt, inarticulate, moody, and with a bad reputation to boot. But he also needed nurturance, a quality Ruth had in abundance (and had shared with everything from dolls to pets).

Ruth's parents decided that to react to Jesse with full disclosure would drive them together, but to say nothing might give tacit approval to the relationship. When the bonds deepened and appeared heading toward a sexual involvement, Ruth's parents decided to engage in the kind of discussion that focused on the meaning of commitment, and the nature of what they considered meaningful between partners. Never mentioning Jesse by name, or giving anything but neutral responses to Ruth's questions about whether or not they liked Jesse, they were successful in conveying their values without driving their daughter away.

Ruth stayed with Jesse longer than they hoped she would, and even today she has a fondness for him. But they are no longer a couple, and Ruth appreciated the help and clarification her parents provided, even though it was not a happy time in their life together.

Adolescent sexuality is not a simple subject. Just when you think you've fielded one line drive, like "How many times did you score in high school, Dad?" (you can deflect that one by saying either, "When you're older and a full adult, then I'll talk to you about my adolescent sex life," or "Do you really want to know?"—most youngsters do not want to know), you've got another shot coming right at you: Your son tells you that if he can't spend time alone with his girlfriend in your house, then he'll just go someplace else. If your values are clear, you may have determined that this is a non-negotiable issue, and so you may say, "I'm sorry, but I am the adult in this house, and I'm uncomfortable with that kind of behavior here. There will be no stuff like that here or anywhere else, and that's that."

Jimmy enjoyed a close relationship with his father, one that each was proud of and wanted to continue. Each knew that there was an unusual openness between them. They could talk about almost anything—and often did.

But when Jimmy asked his father how many women he slept with before he married Mom—and how many he had slept with since he'd been married—Jim Sr. felt that an invisible boundary line had been crossed. If he were to answer those questions honestly, more information than he wanted public would have been disclosed. However, not being forthright with his son was not the style of their relationship either.

What Jim Sr. did was use the opportunity to create an important lesson for Jimmy. "Not every question should be answered just because it has been asked," he said. "And sometimes secrets are not rude, but helpful. Each of us has some information that is best kept just inside ourselves. If everyone told everything about everything, a lot of feelings and other people would be damaged and hurt.

"This is one of those cases," he continued. "I love your mother and do not want or wish to be married to another woman, but we both met as adults and therefore had a long history of knowing and meeting people before we met. We both agreed that it would not be helpful to each other to share every detail of those relationships. And I feel the same way about your questions, son."

Jimmy understood what his father was saying. And that exchange enhanced, rather than destroyed, the closeness that they felt for one another.

Dealing with sexuality is often touchier than with other problem areas of adolescence; the emotions dredged up by visions of breasts and babies are a bit more intense than those involving veal and vegetarianism. But if the emotions are stronger, so too are the rewards for parents who help perpetuate, positively and meaningfully, one of the most wonderful and complex mysteries known.

8 | Alcohol/Drugs: Issues of Substance

Like sex, the issues of drug and alcohol use and abuse are weighty and complex. Like sex, they are issues loaded with potential problems, double standards, shades of gray, and heated emotions.

But unlike sex, substance use does not always take place behind closed doors. While sex in our society is sold primarily through suggestive images that leave much to the imagination, alcohol consumption is portrayed glamorously—and explicitly—in the media. Beer manufacturers sponsor sporting events, museum exhibitions, and rock concerts; the sophisticated ads of wine and spirits producers appeal to upscale young consumers. Even casual drug use has received favorable treatment in contemporary movies and novels.

Drugs such as marijuana and cocaine are, of course, illegal, but the line between those substances and, say, tobacco, alcohol, and diet pills is razor-thin and none too clear. The opportunity for adolescents to charge "hypocrisy" or "double standard" arises whenever we talk about substance abuse, and it is a chance they seldom pass up. Teenagers are, after all, at an age when their hypocrisy detectors are working overtime.

As are their impulses. Adolescence is a time of experimentation in many areas and, unfortunately, substance use is one of them. Although you may try to prevent experimentation with drugs and alcohol, you must face reality and understand that you probably will be unsuccessful.

As a 1990s parent of an adolescent, you must assume that some night, probably when you're least prepared for it, your son will stagger through the front door doing a very bad imitation of the Virginia reel. You must assume that some afternoon, probably when you're feeling most on top of the world, you will get a call from a neighbor that begins, "I hope you don't think this is none of my business, but if it were *my* daughter *I'd* hope someone would tell *me*. Well, I thought you'd want to know that Noelle..." And you must assume that, when you find matches and rolling papers in your son's underwear drawer, he is *not*—despite what he would have you believe—"keeping them for a friend."

Adolescents are experimenters. Even the "straightest," most dependable and reliable kids will at certain points in their adolescence be overcome by their impulses. They will succumb to peer pressure, to the blandishments of billboards and pop heroes, to the adolescent myth of invincibility.

But assuming that experimentation will occur does not mean you must accept it. While it is true that youngsters across all racial and social groups—jocks, motorheads, skaters, 4-H'ers—experiment with substances, it is also true that substances become a way of life for only some adolescents. Some teenagers form peer groups and cliques *around* drugs and alcohol; these substances become their raison d'être, rather than serving as occasional props in otherwise rich, varied lives.

So it becomes your job to prevent the occasional experiment from sliding into dangerous abuse. You must be aware of and differentiate between the signs of experimentation and abuse. You must learn to tell the difference between a teenager who "goes to lots of parties" and one who "parties all the time." (The word "party" has evolved into a verb, meaning to get high.) You must be able to accept very occasional experimentation as part of an adolescent's rites of passage, while doing your utmost to make sure it does not deteriorate into constant, destructive abuse.

What constitutes "experimentation"? It is isolated; it is occasional; it does not involve such highly dangerous drugs as crack, cocaine, LSD, heroin, or angel dust. It is a one-time or once-in-awhile foray into the world of illicit substances that develops no pattern, and has no predictive value for future behavior. It is also done in such a way that youngsters often manage to get themselves caught. Adolescents who experiment with liquor may take their parents' beer or replace their vodka with water. This behavior is bound to work against them at some point; most parents are perceptive enough to notice missing liquor.

A youngster who talks openly to you about a friend or neighbor's substance abuse might also wish to be caught. Listen closely when your adolescent confides in you about someone else. Is he actually saying, "I've tried it too. Help me stop"? Only you can answer that question. This is particularly so because parents often have a vested interest in seeing their children in idealistic, sin-free ways—not as the troublesome, experiment-prone boys and girls they sometimes are.

What is the proper parental response to experimentation? "Lance, we both know you've been drinking our whiskey" is a good way to begin; it helps shift the discussion away from "whether," and on toward "what" and "why." An adolescent who has been experimenting is apt to admit he's been caught; the further along the continuum of use, abuse, and addiction he is, the more likely he will be to deny it.

Youngsters who are experimenting will leave evidence of their work, because they want to stop and be stopped. They will not deny what they've done; they may even without knowing it, welcome parental intervention as a way of relieving peer or societal pressure. They want to do the right thing and an effective parenting response of setting limits and reinforcing family values will help them do it.

"We don't want our 14-year-old to drink, You're not ready to deal with alcohol and its consequences. Period." is all you should have to say. Your word choice, your tone of voice, even your body language, all should indicate with complete certitude that this is not one of those earring or curfew issues; it is a nonnegotiable—in fact, a nondiscussion—item. Your objective is to set up situations allowing your adolescent to emerge—a few years from now, when the period of experimentation is over—relatively unscathed and fairly "together," proudly embracing an intact set of values.

Most parents find this is a difficult objective to achieve. The volatile incidents and ambiguous situations pop up with greater frequency in a discussion of substance use than perhaps any other area of adolescent development. There are so many minefields, so many substances to experiment with and abuse, that it is difficult to lay down hard and fast rules for you to follow. But in any discussion of "experimentation," certain themes do pop up with regularity.

Take the issue of drinking and driving, for example. How many times have you been tempted to say—or have actually said—"I don't want you drinking now—it's illegal until you're 21. But if you do get drunk, please just give me a call. I'll pick you up, no matter what time it is."? And after you said it, haven't you felt confused by the mixed messages you were sending, and wondered if your adolescent was even more befuddled than you?

We agree with the aim behind the statement. It follows from our previous advice that you acknowledge experimentation, without condoning it, but we suggest you strengthen it a bit more.

"I don't want you to experiment," you might begin. "Alcohol is illegal, and the penalties if you get caught are severe. But I know you're at a stage in your life when you *might* experiment, and be unable to adhere to the rules and values I've set for you. And you might find yourself about to get in trouble because of your experimentation."

"If that happens," you could continue, "then call me. I love you, and I'll come get you. But the rules still apply, and I expect them to be followed."

You cannot shortcut this type of message; you need to send it clearly, in its entirety. The message we've just outlined does many different things. It conveys an understanding of your adolescent's developmental stage (important for him to know you understand him), while at the same time demonstrating your firmness and resolve. You've reiterated that you love him and will be there when he needs help, but you've left no doubt that if he messes up, he will suffer the consequences.

USE AND ABUSE

Such a statement may work with an adolescent who is experimenting with substances, but what about one who is abusing them? How can a parent tell the difference, and what can be done about it?

Abuse of substances involves more of a *pattern* than experimentation does. Substances are used more frequently; the peer group reflects similar substance-oriented values; other family and social rules are broken, besides those concerning substances. There is often a drop in school grades, accompanied by a noticeable decrease in motivation.

This is a drastic problem, one that calls for a drastic response. Parents can begin by approaching the adolescent and saying, "We think we see a problem developing, and we want to help you solve it." This provides an external control. Remember, one of your tasks is to impose order on unordered behavior. Helping an adolescent solve the problem may lead to intervention by a therapist, other professional, or through a twelve step program.

The problem might also be solved through the imposition of random urine testing in the home. We've seen this work recently, on a number of occasions. This, too, is a form of external control.

And if your adolescent counters with, "What about Dad and his three martinis every night?" That may be a valid point, but you cannot allow yourself to be sidetracked by it. "That's a separate issue," you may say, "and we're not going to talk about it right now." Period. Sentence. Paragraph. You're in charge now, which any time you're discussing adolescent substance use and abuse, you must be.

On the other hand, this may be a time for parents to listen to their adolescent very carefully, and stop and evaluate their own drinking habits. A family that is going to confront an adolescent with their concern about alcohol use must also be willing to confront their own values in this area, and perhaps alter their own habits after doing so.

Studies have repeatedly shown that a high percentage of teenagers are involved in some way with alcohol. This means that most families today must look carefully at their own definition of acceptable drinking, and what messages they're sending their teenager. In some cases, an adolescent's drinking may serve as a bellwether for alcohol abuse elsewhere in the family. Adolescents often see things their parents don't, especially in this area. One possible meaning of a teenager's drinking behavior may be that he is worried about the excessive drinking of someone he admires and loves.

And if there is, in fact, a substance abuse problem within a family, that information must be communicated to the adolescent. Pretending that all is well when it actually is not does everyone a disservice—especially the adolescent, who receives a message that alcohol abuse is not a problem that should be faced square on.

Miriam, the daughter of an alcoholic, married Sam, who turned out to have a drinking problem. She had promised herself she would never marry an alcoholic, but when she met Sam twenty years earlier he did not seem to drink to excess. Sam's problem surfaced early in their marriage, but was denied by everyone until their son John became a heavy and frequent drinker at 15. He took his first drink as an experiment when he was 13.

Sam, a heavy smoker, was strongly committed to his successful electrical contracting firm, which employed twenty-five people. His drinking began before he arrived home; it did not result in obnoxious behavior, and seldom attracted attention. But when he got in the house, he would have two or three drinks before dinner, then wine with his meal, and he would "go right to sleep" soon after he finished eating.

The family accepted this pattern as normal for Sam. He had plenty of stress on the job, Miriam would rationalize; besides, he was not missing work or suffering from hang-overs. Although Sam did not always remember what hap-pened from dinnertime on, the family—which included, besides Miriam and John, son Todd (17) and daughter Jenny (11)—had all gotten used to his nonavailability. As is often the case with alcohol abuse, no one talked about the problem. If someone outside the family raised the subject, the family members denied it, and the subject was considered closed.

Todd had experimented with many different substances, including tobacco, alcohol, marijuana, and cocaine (and probably others his parents did not find out about), but showed no signs of being in trouble with any of them. He was a good student and athlete, and had friends who seemed like nice, responsible teenagers.

He confined his beer drinking to weekends, and did not get "wasted." Todd seemed to be getting through the experi-mentation stage without too many scars; he showed none of the symptoms of alcohol abuse (daily use; obsessive think-ing about and planning use; poor attendance and failing grades at school; argumentative, hostile, defensive behavior; increasing amounts of time spent away from home or in his room) that his brother John had. Except for one incident when he stole a $2 item from a local convenience store, Todd had avoided trouble with the law.

But John, his mother observed, was using alcohol every day; she also thought he was smoking marijuana often. He seemed to have lost interest in school; he was skipping classes regularly, violating curfews, and generally acting irresponsibly. He spent most of his free time in his room, with the stereo blasting. Whenever his mother said anything negative, Jenny "protected" him. John had gotten her to lie and run interference for him.

With his father pretty much out of the picture (except to pronounce occasional ineffective edicts to the children), the full burden of running the family fell on Miriam. She had hoped to be able to ignore the whole problem, because acknowledging her husband's alcohol abuse problem would force it to the fore, and she dreaded what might happen then. (Divorce? Loss of her husband's job or firm? Townwide gossip?)

However, she saw what was happening to John and worried that if she did not step in soon, it might be too late for him—and perhaps for Jenny too, who was close to John and idolized him. She knew what denial of her own father's drinking problem had done to her mother and brother. In fact, she was still trying to deal with it herself. She noticed the glaring differences between Todd's and John's behaviors, and realized that John was in trouble.

Yet when she talked to her husband one morning, the conversation sounded familiar.

"Honey, John came home and had alcohol on his breath again last night," she began. "That's three times this week—that I noticed."

"So what?" Sam replied. "He's just doing what every other kid in that whole school is doing."

"No," Miriam said. "If he's drinking every day, I don't think that's normal."

"Are you saying I'm not normal?" Sam asked. "I drink every day, and it doesn't hurt anyone. I could stop any time I wanted to. What are you talking about anyway?"

Miriam was desperately trying to avoid a direct confrontation over her husband's drinking. "We're not talking about you right now, Sam, although I think we better some time. It's just that John's gotten more and more involved with this bad group. The kids are getting drunk and stoned all the time. His grades are going down. Haven't you even noticed?"

Sam turned to face her, his eyes bulging. "I can see you're overreacting again. Let me talk to him. I'll tell him to cut back a little, if that'll make you happy."

He turned to leave for work, but said something over his shoulder. "And why do you always raise problems when I'm running out the door?"

Miriam could say nothing else. She knew that her family was in deep trouble. She needed to seek help and support; it was not a job she could handle alone. One option was to speak to John's guidance counselor; she could also turn to a social worker, a member of the clergy or her family physician.

Miriam finally decided that the best help would come from Alcoholics Anonymous (AA). They were familiar with such situations firsthand and could help her deal with the problem—and with her fears of dealing with the problem.

An excellent source for information about alcohol use is the National Council on Alcoholism and Drug Dependence. Their toll-free number is (800) 622-2255.

A fine reference resource is the National Clearinghouse for Alcohol and Drug Information. Their toll-free number is (800) 729-6686.

The hotline telephone number for the National Institute on Drug Abuse is (800) 662-4357.

With the possible exception of sexuality, there are few other areas where it is more crucial for parents to examine, comprehend, and refine their own values, and the values they want their children to embrace, than in the area of substance use and abuse.

Double standards abound. Some parents smoke marijuana themselves, either openly or "secretly" (though we can keep very few secrets from teenagers); others don't condone it but look the other way when their children smoke. Some adults rationalize, "I let my kid drink at home for a good reason: so he won't do it anywhere else." Others are alcoholics themselves, yet they continue to lay down highly structured codes of behavior for their youngsters.

At 14, R.J. had already experimented with tobacco, alcohol, and marijuana. He stayed away from everything else and had no desire to use any of the substances he'd tried (except on occasion). His friends were more extensively involved in drugs; but he was not. He didn't need drug involvement to earn his peers' respect; he was a good enough athlete and student to get his positive strokes in school.

Both of R.J.'s parents worked locally: his father as a dentist, his mother as a school secretary. They were involved in their community and were active in a local church. They drank occasionally but claimed to use no other substances.

R.J. and his sister Debbie, 16, were "good kids." Debbie was a bit "funky" (to use her father's affectionate term), but was well-tolerated; offbeat is fine, one family value went, as long as you are performing okay in school, and are not smoking, drinking, or doing drugs. They were two highly functioning youngsters in a highly functioning family; the grandparents and cousins were close, too. Except for one odd uncle who seemed to have gone off the deep political end, the extended family seemed to have no major problems.

In his normal search to find out who he was, R.J. became the family spy. He looked at everyone with microscopic eyes, annoying them all with his constant snooping. He seemed to be searching for any quirks; perhaps if he found them, he'd be able to get away with a little more than he had up to that point. So far, his parents had not had to clamp down on either him or his sister too hard.

One weekend, prying around while his parents were out of town at a wedding, R.J. found some marijuana in his father's sock drawer. He felt shattered, angry, betrayed—what hypocrites!

That was all he needed; he now had permission to act out. He quickly called a friend whom he knew liked to party, and while his sister tried to control what was happening (but could not), R.J. and his friend proceeded to get very, very stoned.

That evening, his parents returned (as R.J. knew they would). They were horrified. Looking at each other, they knew instinctively what was going on, and why ("He found us out!"), but through their intuition honed over two decades of marriage, decided with one glance not to make any admissions or accusations at that point. They knew there was a lot riding on how they would handle the situation of finding their son high on their own marijuana, and their daughter sobbing "It's all your fault."

They called the parents of R.J.'s friend and asked them to come pick up their son. They told R.J. they would talk about what happened the next day, and they pacified and reassured

Debbie as best they could. Then they retreated to their bedroom, where they had plenty of soul-searching to do.

Why were they using marijuana? Was there anything wrong with their private lives, or with their married life? Why did they hide it from their children? These are some of the many questions they asked each other, long into the night.

And they discussed how they would deal with their overwhelming embarrassment, and how they would (if possible) save face with their teenagers.

They agreed to acknowledge their occasional use of marijuana, and at the same time admit they were wrong to do so. They knew they had to reinforce the idea that it was wrong for their youngsters to use the drug, too, and decided that the only way they would be believed was if they stated forthrightly that they had erred.

They did not get much sleep that night, nor did their children. R.J. and Debbie talked for hours, just as their parents were doing.

Fortunately years of trust and healthy relationships, and living according to shared values seldom vanish with one betrayal. In fact, R.J.'s family had openly discussed nearly everything in the past—except this—and when they all assembled around the kitchen table, though no one was looking forward to the morning's discussion, they did have confidence that as a unit they possessed the strength to survive whatever lay ahead.

Parents of adolescents need courage—with a capital C—to stand up for their values and against double standards, if they are to negate the "hypocrisy!" taunts of their teens. If ever there were a time to have the courage to say no, it is when you are confronting an issue of substance abuse.

When a parent discovers a son or daughter is selling drugs, professional and legal help should be sought immediately. At the same time, lines of communication should be kept open with the adolescent, but this is a set of circumstances that requires quick, outside intervention.

Whether we agree with it or not, one rite of adolescence is to test limits. And some members of this '90s generation of adolescents—because of the incredible influence wielded by society, the media, and the entertainment industry—holds substances in some veneration. That's the way today's teens test limits—just as their grandparents tested limits years ago using another substance, tobacco.

The pressures of society cut both ways. Not only do adolescents feel that alcohol and drugs are "cool," but parents worry unduly about how society will view them if they take a strong stand against substance use. What will my son say if I'm the only parent who doesn't let him go to the pre-prom party because there will be drinking? What will the neighbors say if I tell them their daughter had a major league bash when they were in Bermuda? What will the community say if word gets out that *our* daughter has to go to a detox unit, or a rehabilitation clinic?

The answer, of course, is not what your child or the neighbors or the town thinks. It's what *you* think—what you feel and believe and know in the essence of your being. That's why you must take a stand against substance use and abuse—because if you don't have the courage to say no, then no one else will either. If you don't have the courage to face a distasteful situation, if you turn away to avoid a confrontation, or deny warning signs because you can't stand the thought that your kid is abusing drugs, then you are doing more than failing your adolescent, you're also failing yourself. By not holding true to the values you claim to live by, you can make living with yourself very, very difficult.

Sometimes, of course, an abuse-related issue will arise that a family cannot control. An active alcoholic parent cannot serve as an appropriate role model for an experiment-prone adolescent, for example. In such cases, the teenager should be encouraged to seek help from an adult who *can* cope—a program director, counselor, or other appropriate older person. There *are* role models available, when a parent is incapable of proper boundary setting or ordering behavior.

SAYING NO

Despite the good intentions of politicians and others, it may not always be possible for adolescents to "Just Say No" to drugs or alcohol. Scare tactics, though sometimes well meant, can erect stone boundaries, or cast unwavering attitudes in cement. At times what may be needed is a more subtle approach in which the family realizes that impulse-driven adolescents may, at times, indeed say "yes."

But it is important for parents of adolescents to know and maintain the distinction in seriousness between, on the one hand, alcohol and marijuana, and on the other, more dangerous and/or quickly addictive substances such as cocaine, crack, and LSD. Use of such lethal drugs must be confronted and stopped immediately; one does not "experiment" with mind-altering or toxic chemicals.

As this book is written—and, unfortunately, in the foreseeable future—drugs are and will be a moving target. New forms of coke are being synthesized all the time. While *all* use of drugs and alcohol by adolescents is illegal and dangerous and should be actively discouraged, parents must at the same time recognize certain facts of life. For as long as there have been illegal substances, adolescents have experimented with and used them.

A proven and successful parental strategy for dealing with the drug situation involves numbers. One or two parents might consider enlisting other POAs to form a neighborhood or community organization. A network of parental norms and values can be exceedingly helpful in fighting adolescent drug use. For instance, parents can band together to devise rules concerning supervision of teenage parties. It is tremendously difficult to say no to adolescents when peer pressure is involved, but the task becomes easier if other parents are saying the same thing. There is strength and support—even courage—in numbers.

Investigate programs such as Mothers Against Drunk Driving and Students Against Drunk Driving, among others. Make "the courage to say no" a community cry. If you and your neighbors and your neighbors' neighbors, all send the same message, then your adolescent will not feel isolated if he too says "no." You'll be combating the pressure of one peer group with the strength of another, and you will be amazed to find how well that positive pressure works. It performs one more function, too: It helps adolescents structure their own behavior by creating around them a larger structure of adults who have similarly structured their own behavior, and that is one of the primary tasks of parenthood.

Obviously, we cannot detail here every stomach-turning situation involving substance use and abuse, nor can we provide "suggested responses" for each. There are too many variables, too many substances; each individual is unique, as is each incident. However, we would like to mention two—a pair of situations we believe more than a few parents can identify with.

Mark heads to the movies with friends. Suddenly, at 9:45, you receive a call from the police: He is dangerously drunk and his 14-year-old stomach may need to be pumped. Your first reaction concerns his health, but when it becomes obvious he will be fine, you begin to focus on his behavior.

Obviously, now is not the time to begin a discussion with Mark of the evening's events. We advise a one-day—perhaps even two-day—hiatus for all involved. Comments blurted in anger or resentment won't help anyone; remember, as we help adolescents deal with their impulses, we must also control our own.

Perhaps you can begin, after an appropriate cooling-off period, by saying, "You went way overboard, Mark. That behavior won't work; it's illegal and dangerous. What was going on in your life that caused you to drink so much?"

"Dale and Derek dared me," he might say.

"Well, you saw how much you could drink, and what happened when you did."

"Hey, it's Johnnie Walker. You guys drink it all the time," he may counter.

"It's legal for us to drink; it's illegal for you, Mark. You're 14 years old," you point out.

"Okay, okay, I'm sorry, alright? It was stupid. I won't do it again," he says, hoping that will end the discussion.

But you still must make an important point. "I'm afraid you blew it. You won't be going out again for awhile, Mark."

You've hit home now. "But I'll be an outcast!" he wails.

"I understand all the pressure," you say. "It must be rough when Dale and Derek dare you to do something you're not sure you want to do. It's not easy to say no. But we'll help you say no to them, and we'll do it by saying no to you right now. We're sorry you did this, and sorry about what happened, but you knew our feelings about drinking. You blew it." And then you tell him what privileges he's lost.

No shouts, no threats, no recriminations—just a few clear, direct thoughts that leave no doubt in Mark's mind where you stand. You love him, you feel badly for him—but you still intend to make him suffer the consequences of his own impulsive behavior.

A second situation involves Hillary. She's third in her class, plays the oboe, organized the school's recycling program, and is loved by teachers and students alike. Recently she's developed a crush on Bart, who is no one's idea of a good kid. He's a known substance abuser, whom Hillary has decided to "save."

What can a parent do? Allow the odd romance to run its course? Strew anti-drug literature throughout her room? Pack Hillary off to Outward Bound?

As with every such situation, we make the same point: You know your child best. You know better than anyone else why she would be attracted to such an unlikely boy; you know best whether you can talk openly with her.

If you can, you might begin, "Hillary, honey, we know you're seeing a lot of Bart, and we're concerned. We know the, um, type of reputation he has."

"Mom, Dad, you guys don't know the real Bart. Nobody does. It's not his fault, He's really sweet," she pleads.

"I'm sure we don't," you respond, but the discussion never gets beyond that level. Situations involving substance use are difficult enough, but when sex and romance get added to the stew, they become almost unsolvable.

At times like this, it helps to remind ourselves that we cannot confront all bad behavior, nor can we choose our teenagers' friends. In such situations, the best thing you can do is reiterate the same ideals you have been conveying for years.

"We can't follow you around, Hillary," you can say. "You're too old for that. All we can do is let you know that Bart is not welcome in this house. Here's why . . . ." And once again you explain your values to your daughter—not speaking against Bart, but for yourself and your family—and hope that at some point, what you have said begins to have meaning for her. This is just another way of helping your adolescent structure her own values by giving her methods to help maintain her relationships with her peers, while still saying no.

Most issues of substance use and abuse crop up suddenly. The long-running drinking-at-the-prom debate is a far less frequent occurrence than the bolt-from-the-blue "Why does her breath smell like mouthwash at midnight?" question. But if you have been in the habit of setting limits on a daily basis for as long as your adolescent can remember; if life in your home is lived not according to the rhythm of the occasional prom night or big party, but rather on the basis of "You're going out with friends? Be back by midnight. I'll be downstairs when you get back," then you have done a clear, conscientious job of building shared family values. And then, if you're lucky, the times you'll have to deal with substance experimentation, use, and abuse will be few and far between.

9 | Academic Achievement: Over-, Under-, and Anti-

Of all the pressures an adolescent must bear perhaps the heaviest is one we as a society have developed, honed, and raised to an art form: the pressure to succeed—in school, in sports, in life. We have created measures as means of putting value on how successful or unsuccessful we are as human beings. With adolescents, that measure far too often is based on academic grades. Grades are a way of measuring not only an individual student's success but also parental success. Many parents grade themselves on the basis of their adolescent's academic ability as it is measured by others.

This is a dangerous practice. When parents of adolescents allow others to "grade" the success of their families, they may introduce an element that can confuse an established family value system. Academic achievement should be a concern of the student; parental intervention prevents him from taking charge of his own life on his own turf. School is the adolescent's turf, and the job of a parent is to learn to allow that student to handle that turf without interference and judgment.

This pressure comes entirely from us. It is not a normal developmental pressure of adolescence; it is not even a longstanding "traditional" societal pressure. It is a relatively recent addition to the pile of pressures adolescents already face, and we apply it in a number of ways: a barrage of questions about test scores, report card grades, and class rank; conversations about SATs, transcripts, and college visitations; even casual remarks dropped every time a car with a Harvard, Stanford, or Brown sticker drives by.

It's no coincidence that the shift from elementary school to middle or junior high school takes place around the same time as the change from childhood to adolescence begins. At nearly the same moment youngsters trade in their security blanket of prepubescence for the T-shirts and trendy sneakers of adolescence, they are moving from the cocoon of a single classroom, and the warmth of a teacher who knows and coddles them, to a sprawling building crammed with boys and girls hustling from room to room, each class a new experience with a different teacher.

Up ahead, from junior high onward—like an onrushing train with brakes that don't work and a horn that can't quit—looms: COLLEGE!

For the first time, as both students and parents become aware that in a few years a major step into the outside world must be taken, grades become all-important. Letters and numbers are rigidly used to place our children in categories. Cute smily-face stickers and vague "Satisfactory/Needs to

Improve" notes are replaced by stark numbers and unyielding letters. And for the first time, the reality begins to sink in that evaluation by *outside* sources—teachers, guidance counselors, college admissions officers—may have a crucial effect on our youngsters' lives.

This realization occurs at a time of overwhelming change in adolescent life. Where yesterday their biggest decisions were which Nintendo game to play, their biggest challenge kicking a playground ball as far as it could go, today *everything* matters: their social life, changing relationships with parents and siblings, the desire to earn their own money. And on top of that, they are expected to get good grades, because *soon they will be applying to college.*

While all these changes are colliding like bumper cars at an amusement park, we parents are doing a masterful job of sending mixed messages. "All we care about is that you work hard and do your best," we preach, but then we equate A's with hard work, B's with adequate work, C's with poor work, and D's and F's with catastrophes no less awesome than the sun ceasing to shine. We say, "We'll be pleased to see *any* improvement," and when our teenager raises her C up to a B-, we pounce: "See, we knew you could do it. Now that you've proved you can, we expect at least a B+ from you next quarter!"

Adolescents react to such pressure in a variety of ways. Some achieve low grades on purpose; it's one way of rebelling against parents who try to steal the credit for inspiring their children to do well ("Aren't you glad you listened to us and stayed home last weekend to study?"). Others might fall just short of the A's we "know" they're capable of because, deep down, they don't want to go to Princeton, like Dad; they'd rather go to Bard, like George down the street who's a creative writing major there now and loves it. And some youngsters, unfortunately, become so focused on grades as the sole indicator of success or failure that they lose all sight of the fact that education is a lifetime process, rather than a short-term chore. They get "good" grades, and they may end up at "good" schools, but they run a very real risk of becoming unhappy adults, with unrealistic definitions of achievement and success.

When adolescents reach the crossroad where grades become important, and scholastic pressures increase, you must make a conscious decision to pull back. You must shake your head vigorously to clear your brain of misguided notions that how well or poorly your children do in school, or what university does or does not accept them, is a reflection of how successfully or unsuccessfully you have performed your role as a parent.

An adolescent's education is the responsibility of the adolescent. You can, indeed should, provide the basic framework for that education: a good desk, decent lighting, and today a computer wouldn't hurt. You can even open the book to the right page, if you feel you must.

But you cannot force knowledge into an adolescent's head. It simply can't be done. Your expectations, and your child's reality, are two separate things. You cannot expect to instill your own dreams in your child's heart—no matter how fervently you feel "but it's for his own good!" It is fruitless even to try.

Adolescents instinctively know that they must gain autonomy from their parents, and they know that they can do this in part by turning deaf ears to their parents' educational pleas. In the struggle for independence, academics can be a strategic battleground, and youngsters hold the most powerful weapons. They have far more power than adults realize to work hard, or not work at all, in class or at home. In fact, grades are one of the few areas in which adolescents hold power in their relatively powerless world, and at times they don't hesitate to use that power.

Richard held such power. His parents were both college graduates, the first in their own families to attain that status. His father owned and operated a successful business, and his mother had created her own career track in a large public relations firm. He was the oldest of three children and a bright, competent student from the moment he entered school to the time he completed eighth grade. All through those early school years, both parents spent a fair amount of time discussing the glory of an Ivy League education, and how much difference it could make in an individual's life.

When Richard entered high school, he was comfortably established on the honors track. His first marking period produced the expected A grades, but by the middle of the second term they had slipped to mostly B's. By the end of ninth grade he was making B's and C's. Academics became a family battleground, and during Richard's sophomore year his parents spent hours cajoling, pushing, and pressing for higher marks. Richard responded with sharper and sharper resistance.

He read prodigiously, ran a small, money-making computer repair business on his own, and was a guard on the basketball team. But he spent an infinitesimal amount of time doing homework, and in class slid by with the minimum attention possible. By the end of the year, with C's and D's in hand, Richard won the war. His parents' Ivy League hopes were dashed.

In Richard's junior year, with Ivy League dreams ancient history, he began to work again. By the end of the spring, he was once more a straight-A student. When he met with a college counselor in the fall of his senior year, she looked at his record, saw the very strong SAT and achievement test scores that attested to his competence as a student, and asked him what had created such havoc during his ninth and tenth grade years.

Looking straight into her eyes, he grinned and responded, "Mrs. Somers, those two years were very tough ones. I was in the heart of my hormonal storm."

So our advice to all parents of adolescents is don't make grades a cause célèbre. Chances are you'll lose outright, and even if you "win"—even if your child brings home valedictorianish grades—you'll have won but a Pyrrhic victory. You'll have skewed the stakes so sharply that your child will believe that grades are the most important criterion by which a teenager can be judged.

They are not. Far better to show an interest in the *process* of education (e.g., seeking new knowledge) than in the direct outcome of it (grades); far better to emphasize the *goals* of education (expanding your horizons; learning to think critically and question intelligently) than the *measure* of it (the name of your college).

Communication is essential for any parent who hopes to imbue an adolescent with an appreciation of the process of education. And the communication we're advising must be nonjudgmental. When your youngster brings home a "low" grade, try focusing not on the letter itself, but on the meaning behind it: "How do you feel about that mark? Were you pleased? Was it a grade you think you deserved?"

Questions such as these will elicit far deeper, more thoughtful responses than, "I got a C-. Ms. Coven is a witch." Instead, what you may be surprised to hear is, "Well, it's not *that* bad, considering I got started on the report pretty late and finished it in math. But Neil got a C, and I think mine was as good as his." This may lead into a discussion of what differentiates a "good" paper from a "bad" one, a discussion that could have a longer shelf life than one that begins, "I'm sick and tired of C-, C-, C-. You never got anything below a B last year with Mr. Robesford and now this! What the hell's going on with you and this class, anyway?"

It is not easy to let go in this crucial area of an adolescent's life. It is difficult to bite one's tongue and swallow the words "But Sharla won't work at all unless I pressure her. She has plenty of ability. It's my responsibility to force her to work up to her potential. Look at this composition—it's terrible! What am I supposed to do, let her hand it in like this, watch her flunk out, and then end up at Bilgewater Community College?"

These may be valid fears. But they are fears that cannot be spoken, for the instant you place more academic pressure on your adolescent than she already feels, you have lost—if not in the short run, then surely in the long run.

What you can discuss is your opinion of Sharla's composition. Tell her what's on your mind, but add: "Ultimately, it's *your* work, and *you* have to be happy with it. I have my opinion of this paper, but it's not my writing; it's yours. Are *you* satisfied with it?"

Many times an adolescent might show us a weak paper, knowing full well that it needs work. If we ask if she's satisfied with it, and she says no, that *may* provide her with the excuse she's looking for to stay home and work on it, rather than going out with the gang on Sunday afternoon. Or it may not, and her grade may suffer. But either way, she's learned a lesson about the necessity of completing one's work to one's own satisfaction, and of the fact that each of us bears the ultimate responsibility for the consequences of our own actions. That lesson is more important than any single grade, test, or paper.

As it relates to school pressures, being able to say no thus becomes the courage to say, "No, I won't rewrite this for you," or "No, I won't become over-involved in this grade dispute you're having with your biology teacher. See if you can work it out on your own." It is the courage to say, "No, I won't pressure you to get all A's, and compare you to your brother Raiford who did, because grades are not the sole mark of a successful teenager. School is important, and I am interested in and enthusiastic about your work, but not in a judgmental way. Rather, I am as interested in *how* you learn as in *what* your grade is for learning it. It is *your* education —*your* tests, *your* papers, *your* report cards—and I hope for *your* sake that you are learning not only facts and figures, but also how to think and how to learn."

Parents need to incorporate as part of their longer-adolescent-view that all individuals learn differently, and sometimes those who were least successful during their high school years (gradewise, anyway) are most successful in college simply because they've come to understand themselves without interference from the adults they've encountered. It is far more important for an adolescent to figure out how to cope and to develop an interest in learning, than to establish a strong transcript solely so others can judge his or her progress. All progress is not made or indicated by transcript grades.

What better way for you to encourage the weaning process that received such a firm push the day your adolescent heard for the first time those chilling words: "Don't forget. This goes on your college transcript!"

ACHIEVEMENT PRESSURES

School pressures can manifest themselves in a number of ways besides underachievement. We are all familiar with the "anxious achievers": youngsters who do everything perfectly, usually by staying up long hours and spending all day in a state of high anxiety; youngsters who are determined to fulfill every adult's dreams of them. Such anxious achievers have never managed to differentiate which values, actions, and accomplishments are theirs and which belong to others.

This is a deep-seated problem, and if parents identify such behavior in a youngster, they should take the by-now-legendary step backward, examine their own values (and anxiety level), and recognize that the meaning behind the teenager's behavior is a craving for acceptance and nurturance, driven by the belief that grades and college admissions are the primary criteria by which they will be judged and loved.

Emily had been a "pleaser" from birth. She seemed to have a sixth sense about absorbing the desires of the adults in her life, and incorporating her successes to meet those ends. She dotted every "i" and crossed every "t" on the path to transcript heaven. Every waking hour of every single day was spent in one productive activity or another. She held down a job in a copy shop twenty hours a week; she was president of the school social service club, and was photography editor of the school paper. On the days when extracurricular demands kept her going for long, long hours, she stayed up to whatever time was necessary so that she could complete all her homework, and complete it to perfection. She could keep six balls spinning in the air constantly, without dropping any of them. She "did it all," and did it very well indeed.

As the time to consider college approached, Emily's appearance changed. Her ready smile flashed less frequently, and dark circles appeared beneath her eyes. When she met her college counselor she heard, "You can apply to any of the best schools in the country. Where do you want to go?"

At that she began to cry. "It doesn't matter where I *want* to go; it's kind of like where I *have* to go. I want a big, Midwestern university but my parents and all my teachers will hate me if I don't go east to an Ivy, and I don't want to disappoint them."

Some honest conversation is imperative here. "Your grades are terrific," a parent might say. "But I sometimes wonder if you're pushing yourself so hard for your sake—or for mine."

We must remember that we communicate our expectations, hopes, and fears to our children by the way we live our own lives. Our adolescents hear, see, and sense whether we are happy, disappointed, or disgusted with our own achievements, and they know when we are projecting our own emotions onto their lives. So we need to embark on some meaningful communication with our children about these issues: "Do you feel pressure?" we might ask. "Why? Does it come from within you, or from outside?" And then we should take the conversation—nonjudgmentally and realistically—from there.

Besides the underachiever and the anxious achiever, there is what we call the "antiachiever." This is exemplified by the high school junior or senior who has worked diligently all his life, only to slip a few academic notches just as the college application season begins in earnest. It is not a rare occurrence, and we have found in many cases that the change results from increasing emphasis applied by parents on the importance of grades. Adolescent reactions stem from a self-protective instinct. "If I make good grades," they subconsciously think, "then I might or might not get into the colleges my parents are bugging me to apply to. But if my grades drop just a little, then I definitely won't get in—and the blame is on my teachers, not really *me*."

What all these scenarios—the underachiever, the anxious achiever, the antiachiever—share is a misunderstanding of the educational process. Education does not exist solely for grades and college name-dropping at cocktail parties; it is a *process*—a lifelong process, in fact—and it belongs to each individual alone. Education is a growth process; in order for adolescents to grow they must be invested in their own growth process.

Grades are not the only way to measure or evaluate that growth process, nor is academics the only area in which education takes place. In order to feel good about themselves, adolescents must invest some time and energy in something they enjoy and can succeed in. This may be math, science, history, Spanish—but it may also be field hockey, the clarinet, carpentry, or hospital volunteer work. Not every youngster is capable of performing well in the classroom; those who are probably do not find equal success in every subject.

What *is* important harks back to the very soul of this book: family values. One of the primary challenges of POAhood is helping adolescents find and develop those thoughts, talents, and values that are important to them.

Every youngster has some area of expertise or talent; that is a fact. It is the task of parents to get their adolescents to invest time and energy in activities that they enjoy and are good at—work, sports, drama, music, whatever—so that they can receive positive feedback and feel good about themselves. And POAs must be content to let teenagers receive that positive reinforcement on their own, away from the constant hovering presence of parents.

School is important; there's no denying that. But the pressures of school are so overwhelming that parents don't need to add to them. It is far, far better for POAs to help their adolescents achieve success in other, equally important tasks: socialization skills, work skills, hobbies and avocations, and community relations.

School is an adolescent's job. One of the greatest gifts parents can give is to let their youngster perform that job with a minimal amount of parental interference.

10 | **G**reat Expectations II

Motivation issues surrounding overachievement and under-achievement are not confined solely to academia. Different families measure achievement in different ways; pressure can be placed on adolescents in a variety of areas. We're all familiar with the father who wants his son to be a football star, and the trouble it causes when all the boy cares about is his violin; or the mother who enters her daughter in beauty pageants, when the girl much prefers reading novels and writing short stories; or the parents who are classical musicians, but whose son lives only for rock 'n' roll.

Expectations are peculiar things. Parents use them to fulfill their own views of the way the world ought to be.

Parents also see expectations as positive, helpful forces in a child's life—which they often are. But taken too rigorously and repetitively, expectations can be transformed into hammers held menacingly over children's heads. No youngsters like to feel threatened or pounded, day after day, especially over an issue—their own likes and dislikes—that they are in the process of gaining control over.

Ideally, any discussion of expectations should center around how parents can best help adolescents develop their *own* expectations. In other words, how parents can assist their children in getting involved and investing themselves in those activities, pursuits, and endeavors that are both personally fulfilling and socially beneficial. Parents should help their adolescents form realistic expectations *of themselves*, and not impose adult expectations *on* them. If an expectation is more a parental preoccupation than an adolescent's desire, then whose expectation is it, anyway?

For parents, there is a vast gulf between expectations of childhood and adolescence. When children are young, they have no idea what they want for themselves; instead, they try to live up to their parents' expectations of them. Developmentally, that is accurate and appropriate. But when children charge into adolescence, they are no longer bound by their parents' expectations. Now, as they begin to separate from Mom and Dad and seek independence, they must begin to develop their own set of hopes and dreams—their own expectations of themselves.

Joanne was an attractive, bright high school freshman. Well-liked by peers and adults, she was a much better than average student throughout elementary and junior high school. But by the middle of her first year in high school her grades had slipped dramatically, down to steady C's and an occasional D. Yet her teachers continued to find her charming, and because she did not create any problems in the classroom or at home, no one viewed her drop in grades as a problem.

Joanne and her mother, Janice, had lived together for six years. Her parents had been divorced when Joanne was 8, and shortly after that her father moved to another state. She enjoyed a good long-distance relationship with him, talking by phone at least once a week. They saw each other every three months or so. He was supportive, and enjoyed a friendly relationship with his ex-wife—especially in regard to Joanne.

Janice felt very lucky to have such a good and mature daughter. After the divorce, there had been a period of financial difficulties that had only recently eased. Finally, over the previous two years, Janice was able to finish her college education and get a more rewarding—but also very demanding—job. When she was struggling as a mother and student, Janice had been able to count on Joanne to take care of her many chores at home, and to be responsible for her many activities in and out of school.

When Janice was not sure things would work out right, Joanne was there to listen to her mother and support her goals and expectations for the future. Janice was thankful for her support, especially when her friends told stories about *their* daughters.

After the third marking period grades came in—three D's this time, the rest C's—Janice felt it was time to acknowledge to her daughter that there appeared to be a problem. Joanne denied that there was; it was just that the courses were too hard, she said—and besides, how could she be expected to do as well as she did when she was in elementary school? The teachers were new, the school was bigger, there were more things on her mind . . . . Her final comment, which Janice had heard so often, was "Don't worry, Mom. Things'll work out."

Fortunately, this time Janice did not listen to her daughter; she decided to find out for herself what the problem was. She went into school and learned more about the courses, and the expectations the teachers had for their students. When she found there was no real reason that Joanne couldn't do the work at her usual level, Janice knew it was time for another mother-daughter talk.

The problem, she learned, involved Joanne's expectations of herself. When her schoolwork became more difficult and time-consuming she was unable to succeed as she had in the earlier grades with the same amount of time and energy. She expected too little of herself academically and denied the importance of her performance. But with the help of the school and a good deal of discussion (and not a little heated debate), Janice helped Joanne turn her grades—and her self-expectations—around.

Realistically, Joanne was capable of high achievement. But rather than challenge herself, she found it easier to walk away from the responsibilities she had had to assume for so many years. At that point her mother had to reassert control. Thanks to her experiences after her divorce, Janice knew the benefits of education and of having to expect more of herself than she thought she could give.

The divorce brought about a reevaluation of her own values, and it became her job to pass them on to her daughter. She did not expect or demand things from her daughter that were not possible, but she did ask her daughter to have *realistic* expectations of herself, and that is a positive value.

~~~~~~~~~~

Parents must recognize that their expectations, and those of their adolescent, may no longer share common ground; they must acknowledge that that territory is now owned by the teenager. They must support her in her struggle to develop her own identity by telling her, "We see what you're striving for, and it's interesting and good"—even if it's not an expectation they planned on. They must let go of their own insistence that she meet their expectations of her, in favor of helping her discover her own set of expectations and goals. Some of her expectations may be borrowed from their own; others may be quite different—but the important thing is that the adolescent's expectations come from within herself. For that is the only way by which a searching, questioning teenager can grow into a mature, confident adult.

Need further proof? Look at your own life. Do you still have the same expectations for yourself that your parents held for you when you were a child? Do you think you should?

Enough said.

When youngsters don't meet their parents' expectations, parents may develop their own contrary set. Tired of saying, "You should be a lawyer; you're bright, you love to argue, and lawyers make piles of money," parents begin to accentuate the negative: "If you don't do well this year, you'll have no future, you'll never make any money, you'll be a bum."

Whether or not that's an accurate prophecy is irrelevant. When it is made, the results become predictable: Youngsters find it far easier to live up to those negative expectations than to fulfill the positive ones, so they *do* let schoolwork slide; they *do* become a bit bumlike. It is the rare youngster indeed who has the fortitude and confidence to take the negative words of parents as a challenge and say, "Well, I'll show *you* what I can do!" Few Supreme Court justices have ever been forged in the fire of negative expectations.

So what's a parent to do when an adolescent shows signs of following a career path that that parent would not normally choose for that child—or for himself or herself?

Let's take the second part of that question first. Expectation problems often arise when a parent confuses his or her own expectations with what that parent wants—or claims to want—for the adolescent. "I only want what's best for my child" can also be construed as, "This is my second chance to have what's best for me."

But that is a fallacy. Raising an adolescent is *not* a second chance for you to become an adolescent (or a different adult). It's your adolescent's first and only chance to be one. And if you accept our earlier description of adolescence—that it's a time of wondrous *self*-discovery and *self*-development—then you'll realize it's an area that's not big enough for two of you. So someone better butt out, and guess who that someone is?

We are not, rest assured, saying that there is anything wrong with believing, "I want the best for my child." But what is "best" for your child? The answer to that question takes a long time—much longer than the brief years of adolescence—to figure out. And, just as important, the answer cannot be supplied by you, your spouse, or anyone other than the adolescent himself. *He's* the one who must figure out on his own what's best for him, and he can't do it if you're hovering over his shoulder every step of his journey, telling him which way to turn, which direction to move, where to go. He'll be glad to tell you where to go; trust us.

Whose life is it, anyway? It's your teenager's. It's his happiness, his satisfaction, his fulfillment—so let him make his own way there. And if his path to happiness, satisfaction, and fulfillment takes him through the land of sportscasting, modern sculpture, or deck construction—lands you yourself would never travel to—you must never forget that this is not your journey.

John was 12 when his parents first impressed upon him how musically gifted they felt he was. Both John's parents had achieved a "better life" (compared with their parents), but knew that their children (and John was the first) were going to do even better. They would put all their resources behind their children, they said at those times when they discussed the future together—a value they believed was a worthy one. So John had the best music teacher, attended the best summer music camp, and by his freshman year in high school was enrolled in an excellent Saturday morning music school.

While he was doing all this, his grades slipped a bit each high school marking period. Everyone rationalized this; after all, John certainly had a very busy schedule. To his parents, he seemed to be getting along quite well—even though there were no longer any relaxed, friendly discussions at the dinner table. John ate quickly and quietly, leaving to go "study" before the rest of the family had even finished. Taking his plate to the sink, he would rush off and disappear for the evening. He stopped watching television, playing cards—even fighting—with his younger siblings.

Meanwhile, he slowly began withdrawing into a world that was whittled down to two male friends, only one of whom he felt able to talk to about himself and his world. It was with this singular boy, Grant, that John shared aspects of his life: How he had no time for baseball, yearbook, even just hanging around after school. He liked his music, he told Grant—but not that much. He'd rather play music just for fun, he said, but he knew how much it meant to his parents. He talked often about how hard they worked to give him his "opportunity" and "advantages." He knew he was good; he just didn't know whether he wanted to play music the way his mother and father wanted him to.

He told Grant that he would never want his parents and brother and sister to be disappointed in him; that's why he kept going. But he was not happy. He wasn't sure what would ever make him feel good, he said—but he knew he was not happy then.

John was in a quandary. He had been brought up with good values (hard work; do your best; listen to adults because they're experienced; don't waste time or money), and he had learned that, generally, those values work. In addition, he genuinely loved his parents, and he did not want to hurt them.

Yet John was unhappy because his expectations of himself were simply to have a more rounded life, and to experience as much as he could. He knew that his father did not make his career choice until he was out of college, and he saw that his father was now quite happy with his life. His mother was a nurse, and John knew she had to study that in college—but not in high school. John had gotten to know a few professional musicians, and their lifestyle did not intrigue him; he could not see himself playing music for the rest of his life.

So he waited. Outwardly he appeared to do whatever was asked of him, yet inwardly he withdrew more and more.

Initially, John's parents were a bit concerned about his attitude, and his habit of isolating himself from his family. But when they talked with a number of friends, they heard over and over, "It's just a stage. Give him time." And so they did.

The situation turned into a standoff. John stood waiting for something—anything—to happen, while his mother and father stood waiting for his "stage" to pass.

Finally, after John's sophomore grades slipped further, and his behavior at home grew more and more withdrawn (with a new, heavy dose of surliness mixed in), his parents stepped in. They realized that a very important—indeed, perhaps the most important—family value was honesty. In a series of discussions during which honesty was stressed, John finally told his parents that he felt he was being "dishonest" by not living his own life. Their expectation that he do everything he could with his music was creating unbearable pressure, he said, and while he had tried to do what they wanted as best he could, it wasn't working any longer. He told them he knew he was missing out on parts of his life that he wanted to be involved with. He wanted to see if he could excel in other areas besides music.

Together, the three family members began the long and sometimes difficult process of opening up. His parents worked hard to let John know that his opinion was important, and that they wanted to hear it even if it was different from their own ideas. They let him know that, above and beyond everything else, honesty between them was important. And they also let John know that while his music was indeed important to them, it was not at the expense of his well-being, nor at the expense of his place in the life of their family.

Once every member's feelings were out in the open, a compromise was found. John cut back on his music—

especially his activities outside high school. But all agreed it was not something to be eliminated entirely; rather, it was something that could be modified, so he could have time and energy to pursue other activities.

Most importantly, though, together they were able to reinforce to each other the idea that talking honestly was the most important aspect of their relationship—and that honest communication needed to be fostered before any other activity could take place.

Ah but, pipes the devil's advocate: How can a 17-year-old know or have the merest inkling of what's best for him? Doesn't a parent have a responsibility—indeed an obligation —to butt in then?

The answer is no. You simply cannot run your child's life for him. You are not inside his skin; you cannot know as well as he what thoughts lie inside his brain, what dreams lurk inside his heart. Much as you would like to, you cannot impose your hopes and aspirations on your adolescent, no matter how important you believe them to be (or how off-base you feel his are). You cannot *give* your expectations to your teenager; you can only make sure that he finds, develops, and owns his own.

To do that, you must first step back and assess, realistically and categorically, exactly what your own expectations are, and then you must check yourself to make certain you are not imposing them on your child. Rather than projecting your own hopes, dreams, and aspirations on your adolescent, you must assess *his* strengths and weaknesses, *his* likes and dislikes. And then, through an ongoing series of honest discussions, you must help him through the process of searching for, defining, and refining his expectations, so that he ends up living his life, loving what he is doing, for himself—not ruing what he is doing for you.

These discussions must, naturally, occur over a period of time. Adolescents' interests and desires change as rapidly as the weather; only with time will you be able to discern patterns of consistency. Don't be alarmed, worried, or annoyed if those patterns focus on music, and you're a banker, or if the talk keeps turning to sports instead of literature. Listen; ask questions; direct the discussion toward ideas, concepts, and opinions, but don't lecture, yell, or threaten. The reason you are *directing* the discussion is to allow your adolescent to discover his own ideas, concepts and opinions—not simply parrot your own. (And you might even learn that your adolescent has quite a different point of view from your own.)

And above all, don't repeat yourself. Many parents follow the old joke about forcing a foreigner to understand English: If you say it loudly enough and often enough, he's bound to comprehend. So these parents trot out and repeat, loudly and often, the same old chestnuts about success, achievements, expectations. They think that by repeating themselves ad nauseam, they'll get their point across; however, the repetition drives the adolescent bonkers. So he tunes out everything the parent says and instead of absorbing and integrating the parent's message, the adolescent rejects everything that's said.

Whenever you have an overwhelming urge to say something relating to what is, in fact, your own expectations of your teenager—"You haven't practiced the cello in a week"; "Don't you think narrow stripes would make you look thinner?"; "Oh, look—hockey tryouts start next week!"—bite your tongue. Keep quiet, and have faith in your adolescent.

What kind of faith? Faith that you have *already*—over the first dozen or so years of his life—done the job of making your values clear to him. Faith that included in those values are certain expectations you have of him. Faith that he has, from infancy on, absorbed those values and expectations and that now, as he embarks on his difficult adolescent journey—a trek during which he will develop and identify *his own* values and expectations—he will keep, come back to, adopt, and adapt many of those same expectations.

Connor had "the devil" in him. Two years younger than his older sister, he learned at an early age that he was bright, and that his sense of humor, huge smile, and sparkling eyes could get him plenty of places most children could not go, including into the hearts of peers and adults. He breezed through school and got along with everyone—until age 14.

That's when there appeared to be a radical change in Connor, almost overnight. The sparkle in his eyes was still there, and so was his huge smile and sense of humor, but now his behavior appeared to be uncontrolled. The year he was 14 was loaded with confrontations, arguments, and letters—whole letters, not just notes—sent home from school.

Connor's behavior was not terrible—there were no gross breaches of social, civil, or criminal law—but all of those laws were often brushed up against. There were late nights, often with reasonable excuses. His grades in school continued to be good, but he became known as the class "smart aleck"; more than one teacher reported that Connor persisted in disrespectful action. He seemed to be on the phone all day and night (most of the calls were incoming). He needed rides everywhere, every day, and he expected those rides to appear at his command.

He seemed involved in everything going on in his school. When anyone asked why, he was ready with a quick retort. His parents tried grounding him for his indiscretions, and they attempted to talk to him about family values. But the punishments never worked, and the discussions turned into monologues.

When Connor turned 16, his parents debated the wisdom of allowing him to get his driver's license. There was no question of his driving ability; it simply was not clear how responsible he would be. His friends were too numerous to mention, and spanned a range of eight years— including plenty of young adults. But they allowed him to get his license, and were relieved (knock wood) when the family car survived that first year.

At 17, Connor developed a social consciousness and discovered current events. He let everyone know exactly what he thought about everything. If their ideas were in conflict with his, he did not hesitate to let them know how faulty theirs were.

Connor was many things to many people. Some felt he was destined for prison, others for political office; still others felt he would successfully "beat the system" by some semilegal means. Some people still thought he was simply terrific.

His parents had no idea what to expect, from one day to the next. They had known early in his life that Connor would have to arrive at any decision by himself, because that was the way he was. He was going to try everything, and everyone would find that very trying. But the one thing they would not allow him was to breach certain family values: doing things to the best of one's ability, trying new things, and showing respect to those who deserved respect. (Thus his parents silently applauded his rebellion against teachers who did not deserve respect, yet punished him for inappropriate expressions of that disrespect.)

Connor's parents did not try to snuff out the "devil" by smothering it with their expectations, beyond saying that Connor would have to be responsible for both his successes and failures. They never excused his behavior, but they tried to understand him and keep him from hurting himself seriously—and from hurting others. It took a great deal of discussion, many hours of argument, and plenty of effort. But because Connor's parents loved him, and he loved them (as best an adolescent can), they all grew through the trying times. Today they enjoy each other as adults, and share many stories about Connor's adolescence.

So continue to talk to your adolescent about expectations, but frame the discussion in such a way that you talk in terms of family values, rather than things. For instance, discuss the value of having expectations, rather than zero in on precisely how your child's expectations differ from yours. Chat about the benefits of work, such as satisfaction, fulfillment, contribution to society, financial rewards, prestige. Discuss hopes and dreams. For example, ask your daughter why she is attracted to horseback riding; don't dwell on the high cost of maintaining a horse. She will learn about high costs all by herself—but you will learn about her (and perhaps even about yourself) by talking about the joys of horseback riding.

Don't be afraid to discuss values as they relate to "real life" experiences. You can talk until you drop about the value of honesty, but when that first tape appears in your son's room that obviously wasn't bought by him, it's time for you to initiate a discussion of the value of honesty. You might even have to go beyond talking, and accompany him back to the store he swiped it from. But whatever you do, do it in the context of a discussion—about family values, and the fact that yours go against the prevailing teenage value that "everybody does it."

These discussions of expectations form a process, similar to the process of education we discussed in the previous chapter. Earlier, we cautioned parents not to focus on the grades themselves, but instead on education as an ongoing process. Now, we add the advice that you should focus not on your own expectations of your adolescent, but rather on the process of helping him define his own expectations of himself, as he defines himself.

Adolescents experiment with values; they try them on for size. And even as they speak those values out loud, they are not necessarily embracing them. Adolescents do not make definitive statements about values; instead, they explore them. And as they explore, it is up to their parents to realize that because teenagers' values may shift, the adults should neither overreact nor underreact.

It is not an easy process. Expectations, which arise naturally from values, are difficult things to define, develop, and achieve. What ultimately makes them so satisfying is that they belong to each of us alone. Self-expectations allow adolescents to create their own values and goals. They are part of the process of developing a healthy self-view, which is based on the ongoing development of values and realistic expectations. No one else can impose expectations on us, or force us to live up to expectations we don't hold. No one at all.

11 | **S**eparation and Independence: Letting Go—Both Ways

Sexuality and substance abuse are dramatic issues for parents of adolescents. Pregnancy, venereal disease, alcohol, marijuana—mention any of these beauties, and you've got an attentive audience of parents hanging on every single word.

But separation and independence are far less titillating subjects. Few parents understand that the stresses caused by a teenager's first job, or by an impending move to college, are just as real and confusing as those created by experimentation with sex and substances. And fewer still realize that those stresses are felt just as strongly by the parent as by the adolescent.

On reflection, of course, parents may recognize that separation and independence are issues fraught with just as much uncertainty, worry, and potential for family disruption as any other situation involving teenagers. In fact, they've been issues far longer than, say, sexuality and substance use; they date back to the instant your child was born. At that moment, as he used all his energy and resources to separate from his mother's womb, he—and you—faced the initial challenge of independence. And you and he have been confronting that challenge ever since.

The first challenges are exciting ones. The day your daughter began to crawl, she was no longer dependent on others for locomotion; when she began to walk, she also began to venture out on her own. Another milestone occurred the first time she did not cling to you when strangers entered the room; then there was the first day of kindergarten, the first time she slept at a friend's house, the first time she left for summer camp.

Look now at all the separation situations we've just listed. Except for a very few—the first day of kindergarten, for instance—they are randomly occurring events. Different youngsters are ready for different separation steps at different times; no two children share the same progression. It is impossible to set an exact timetable for childhood development.

So, too, for adolescence. There are 13-year-olds who date, and 17-year-olds who don't; there are 14-year-olds who hold down steady jobs, and 18-year-olds who don't know how to look for one. There is no clear-cut age at which an adolescent *should* do any of these things which, by the way, are important and necessary steps down Separation Lane, heading out toward Independence Road.

One problem with discussing separation issues is that our society—unlike many others—blurs the line between dependence and independence. Today, fewer and fewer rites of passage signify, "Yesterday, you were a child. Today, you are a man/woman." Gone are most specific ceremonies marking entrance into adulthood; all that remain are such amorphous milestones as the first driver's license, the cutoff point between "PG" and "R" rated movies, high school graduation, and voting privileges. And most issues of separation are even more fuzzily defined than those; they vary widely, depending upon such outside influences as family and community.

Bruce was the younger of two children. Shortly after he began high school, his father died. His mother, who had never worked (and still did not have to, thanks to generous benefits received from her husband's insurance), continued to maintain the family and household as it had always been—close-knit, with plenty of sharing. Bruce's older sister, Cammy, was a bright and competent student. She had just gone off to a top-notch college when Bruce entered his senior year of high school.

Bruce, who also had a very good high school record, began to think about his choice of college. He would not consider Cammy's school, but selected an equally well-known place for himself. His college counselor and his mother insisted that he add two other schools to his list, which were almost equally "name game" but not quite as selective as the first.

That fall, everything related to college applications was late. After procrastinating for weeks, Bruce finally completed his early decision application moments before it had to go in the mail. He was deferred by the school for decision to the April pool. Again, at the last possible second, he mailed in his other two applications.

Bruce maintained his grades throughout his senior year, but the stress he felt was obvious to all who knew him. No words about "many colleges can be the right one for you; no need to focus on one special place" alleviated his anxiety. However, he denied feeling anxious about anything at all, and when a counselor suggested he might be concerned about leaving home and his mother, Bruce downplayed that possibility. He doggedly worked long (and often disorganized) hours to keep his grades together, his stress notwithstanding.

Bruce's early decision deferral became a January acceptance for the following winter. He also was accepted by the two other very respectable institutions, and chose one of them. He left in September, trailing a flurry of last-minute details.

Bruce worked hard that first fall, and earned three As and one B. He spent time in the library, and when he wasn't there or in class he was in his room. He called home at least five times a week and continued to say "I'm fine"—though he sounded frantic.

In November he wrote to the school that had been his first choice, and told them he would be coming in January. He told the school he was attending that he would not be back for spring term because he was not happy with the social life.

When Bruce returned home for Christmas, he told his mother he did not want to be at either school next semester, because January was the worst time to enter anywhere, and besides there was an Ivy League school he really wanted to attend, which he would apply to for the following fall. He would just stay home until he heard from them, but meanwhile he would tell the January school he would be there in

September and would take courses in a community college near home until he heard from his new first choice.

Bruce took one course at the local college. He slept long hours but seemed to be glad to be home, and his mother was glad to have him back. But that application to the Ivy League school never got out before the deadline. In April his mother finally encouraged him to seek professional help; she, too, began to see a therapist.

By summer Bruce was taking two courses at the local college, and was working part time. The following year he took a full course load, and filed his application for fall at his original "real choice" on schedule. Both Bruce and his mother worked hard at resolving their feelings about letting go and beginning their separate lives. Bruce was accepted at his final first choice school and went off with relative ease that next September.

With the separation process less clearly defined than ever, it is far more difficult for parents and teenagers to understand *how* to treat the stresses of separation that bubble underneath the surface of adolescence. There are few clear guidelines, because there are few clear separation issues. Interestingly, that's one of the reasons the college process is so stressful—because it IS one of the true, recognizable demarcation lines.

Yet virtually every issue of adolescence—clothes, friends, curfews, whatever—involves to some degree the natural desire of youngsters for independence and their parents' natural inclination to worry about how they'll fare all alone out there in the adult world.

GROWING APART TOGETHER

One of the major tasks of adolescence is for teenagers to become more independent, and for parents to let them. They need to learn how to manage time, money, work, and relationships by themselves, because they will be responsible for doing these things for the next several decades. They must forge their own, separate school life, social life, family life, and work life, and they must learn how to prioritize them. This is a fundamental function of adolescence—one they have been preparing for for more than a decade. Now that the rehearsal is over, the parents must let the show go on, without them.

Issues of separation and independence cut both ways. Not only are adolescents breaking the thread that binds them to their parents, but their parents must let the thread slip away, and not try to bring their child back in. Certainly, the task is just as wrenching for the parents as it is for the adolescent.

Parents of adolescents are at least as worried about independence as are adolescents themselves. A mother who does not have to wake her daughter for school, fix her breakfast and lunch, and then pick her up afterward, may sense that the "job" she has performed so well for so many years—and with it her "usefulness"—has come to an end. The father whose son buys his own car, so he no longer needs to borrow Dad's for dates, may suddenly feel old, and headed toward the family scrap heap.

To see adolescents functioning relatively successfully *on their own* is to acknowledge that they are operating under their own power. Family roles, outside relationships, and societal functions are changing, and quite naturally, it's the older folks who tend to resist the change. Just as in a company or organization none of us consciously sets out to diminish or de-emphasize his or her own role, so too as POAs do we subconsciously try to keep the family power structure intact, even when it is changing before our eyes.

That's why "the courage to say no" assumes enormous importance in this chapter. Parents of adolescents must say no a thousand times to themselves. They must help their child function independently, not foster dependence—and to do that, they must first say no to their own desire to maintain the familial and familiar status quo.

Resisting your own desire to keep things as they were is an anxiety-provoking task. You feel the normal worries about your youngster—will she perform adequately in her new job? what if he gets lost on his way to the college interview?—but with added stress: The gnawing feeling that you're not parenting correctly if you're not there with your child, every step of the way. To have parented one way for years and then find yourself being phased out of a job, can be disconcerting. But it's a fact of parenting life: Parenthood, like Detroit's cars, means planned obsolescence.

Damian, a high school junior, has a class that meets at 7:40 every morning. Damian's parents believe that if they do not wake him, he'll never get there. So each morning, at 6:30 sharp, Dad opens his door, shakes him awake, then retreats downstairs to help prepare breakfast.

But Damian does not get up. He falls right back asleep, and for the next forty-five minutes his mother scurries between kitchen and bedroom, doing her best to get her son ready for school.

Mom and Dad use every trick in their bag to make sure Damian reaches school on time: Alluring breakfasts are borne in on trays so when time is tight he won't leave home undernourished. He is driven to school each time he is late. They even consider buying him a used car so he won't have to rely on buses or friends for transportation.

The end result, of course, is that Damian remains a procrastinator par excellence. Not only does he get to sleep late, he also gets breakfast in bed, and a guaranteed ride to school. He's living the life of Riley, and is doing it with the implied consent—in fact, the active assistance—of his parents. They are perplexed and overwhelmed. An inordinate number of evenings are spent discussing the issue of Damian, and how he should be treated.

They have reasons for their behavior, of course. "Damian already has sixteen tardies," they explain to friends and neighbors who are amazed at their routine. "If he's late four more times, he'll flunk English. We're sorry, we just can't let that happen. Think how that would look on his college transcript!"

To which we say: Think how it will look on his *life* transcript to grow up without learning how to function independently or to suffer the consequences of his own actions. Think how Damian's parents are stifling his drive to live on his own, to learn how to make good decisions and bear with bad ones. Think how much more beneficial, albeit more worrisome and difficult, it would be for them to ignore Damian's snores when 6:30 rolls around.

If Damian does not get up in time, if he spends too much time making his own breakfast; if he misses the bus or his friends can't wait for him, and he cannot find alternate transportation, what will happen then?

For starters, Damian might hit the magic "20" tardies in English. In accordance with well-known school rules, his grade might get lowered, perhaps all the way to an F. He might have to attend summer school, or take an extra English course senior year. He might feel mad, frustrated, belligerent, or upset.

He might also grow up. Perhaps he will work his way up to nineteen tardies, then suddenly realize that Mom and Dad are serious and swing into action. He may begin to set his alarm for 6:15, learn to eat fruit rather than eggs for breakfast, figure out how to make his lunch the night before, find out how to call a cab if he misses the bus, and discover how much more expensive taxis are when the money comes out of his own pocket.

Then again, perhaps he won't. He may *want* to do all those things, yet be unable to get his act together well enough to pull it off. Despite his best intentions, he may be late to English twenty times and may suffer the consequences he'd worked relatively hard to avoid.

That's when—if Damian were your son—you'd have to close your eyes, feel bad for the kid, and take solace from the fact that, distressing as it seems, you're doing your part to turn your boy into a free and self-sufficient man.

Why, after all, do you think he's been acting this way? Do you believe there is an underlying motivation for his sluggishness, or do you think he is simply unable to wake up with the rest of the world?

If you've read this far, you must by now agree with us that "all behavior has meaning," and the meaning here is that Damian is testing himself. He is testing whether he actually is ready to handle his own responsibilities independently. When his parents wake him up every morning, the meaning of their behavior becomes, "No, baby, you're not ready."

At this stage in life, an adolescent is apt to protest loudly how ready he is for independence. "Leave me alone! I'm not a baby! I can handle it!" That same adolescent is then apt to turn around and demonstrate dramatically how *un*ready he is to handle that particular situation—at which point the parent jumps in to bail him out. This fosters the dependency the adolescent has just declaimed so loudly against, and the complex cycle of dependence-qua-independence continues.

This is a typical cycle in the growth process, and it's one that cannot be fixed by adolescents; it's not their job, and besides, they are not even aware of what's happening. It falls rather to parents of adolescents to consciously recognize the stumbling block to independence, and to say clearly and forcefully, "I'm letting you have your independence. From now on it is your responsibility to wake yourself up, make your own breakfast and lunch, and get yourself to school on time. I don't care how you do it, but it's *your* job to do it. I'm no longer going to be responsible for that aspect of your life."

In our experience this type of approach works, despite the frightening thought that along the road to independence adolescents may cross the center strip, perhaps even spin out. But it's the only way they can learn to drive that road. It can't be any other way.

PROMOTING INDEPENDENCE THROUGH WORK

Of all the ways adolescents can achieve independence, one of the best is through work. When teenagers take a job, they are forced for the first time to relate to an adult who has no previous connection with them, either through family or school. They are valued by that adult strictly on the basis of performance; in return, they are compensated with money (or in the case of volunteer work, gratitude). Your daughter's adult employer does not check back with you every time she makes a mistake, nor is he likely to praise you when she performs well. Her job is her own, and so is her success or failure in it.

As a parent of an adolescent, you should promote work, whether in the form of a paying job or volunteer work. By so doing, you will be promoting commitment, responsibility, and independence. But your relationship to your adolescent's job must end where the time clock begins. If your daughter messes up at work, stay out of it; let *her* suffer the consequences (assuming, of course, that she does not work at a nuclear power plant). If she is having trouble with a boss or co-worker or with tasks and responsibilities, have the courage to say no to your own natural impulse to interfere and rescue. Instead, let *her* solve her own problems.

This does not mean that you have to remain oblivious to the problem. You should let her know you are available for support, talk, and problem-solving guidance. In fact, problems at work could be an excellent starting point for an important discussion about the fact that life is an adventure filled with good bosses and bad bosses, fun jobs and dreary jobs. But you must take care to limit your comments; in the end, your daughter must solve her problem on her own, in her own way.

Jeff had to solve his problem on his own, too. He was a 17-year-old who was holding down his first regular job at a dry cleaners; his only previous work experience involved sporadic lawn mowing, snow shoveling, and occasional baby sitting, all around his neighborhood. He got the dry cleaners job through his high school guidance office. He liked the steady money; the fact that it could turn into a "work study" unit, with high school credits, also contributed to his decision to take the offer. He knew his boss, Mr. Stone, because his family often patronized the establishment.

One afternoon Jeff's mother saw him leaving the house wearing shorts. Realizing he had been due at work half an hour earlier, she asked where he was going and why he wasn't at work.

"No problem, Mom," Jeff said airily. "Billy's covering for me. I told him everything he needs to know."

Jeff's mother was aghast. Billy was Jeff's none-too-reliable best friend, and had never worked in a dry cleaners, or anywhere else, before.

"Did you tell Mr. Stone?" she asked.

"Mom, I told you, it's no big deal. It's a nice day, I'm going waterskiing at the lake, and Billy'll do just fine. Don't butt in; it's none of your business."

Jeff's mother resisted her parental urge to nix his trip to the lake. She pointed out (swiftly, since Jeff was already halfway out the door) why she thought waterskiing was a peabrained idea—he had obligated himself to work at the dry cleaners; he needed the money to pay back a loan on his new stereo; he had never cleared this with Mr. Stone, who no doubt would be stunned to see the untrained Billy walk through the door—but ultimately she let him make his own decision.

When Jeff appeared at the dry cleaners the following afternoon, Mr. Stone was not the smiling shopowner Jeff knew from childhood. He angrily but quietly explained to Jeff his view of the responsibility of work: The job was a contract between the two of them, and he expected to pay Jeff—not Billy or anyone else—for work performed. Further, if there were to be any changes in that "contract," they had to be mutually discussed and agreed upon.

Mr. Stone told Jeff that he had broken that contract, and, as a result had showed that he was not ready to work. Jeff was stunned. He had never been fired before and had never imagined that this would be one of the consequences of going to the lake. He assured Mr. Stone it would never happen again.

"I'm sure it won't," Mr. Stone said. "And it definitely won't happen to you here, because I'm not going to change my mind. I really am sorry. I'll have your paycheck ready for you tomorrow."

The first firing is often traumatic, but it can also be an enormously positive moment in a teenager's life. It can offer an opportunity for a fruitful discussion on how, when, and why people of any age get canned. That's the discussion Jeff had with his mother when he returned home that afternoon, and it was a discussion Jeff remembered when he began job hunting the following day.

Throughout this chapter, we have assumed that the goals of adolescents and their parents are one and the same; that they are not working at cross purposes. We assume that adolescents want to become active players in the "real world," and that their parents want their children to succeed in it.

POAs must be aware that allowing their adolescents to separate and become independent is equally important for both generations. There will come a time when your son decides he does not want to do everything with you and his siblings, and you should recognize that time when it occurs. That does not mean he should be given carte blanche to do as he pleases—"Oh, you don't want to go to England with us on vacation? Well, you're 15; I guess you can stay home alone for three weeks!"—but it does mean that you should be sensitive to his resentment at being forced to spend every waking minute with his family. Thus, when he asks if he can go to Soho instead of the Tate with you one afternoon, you discuss with him your valid concerns—How will you get there? What kinds of things do you think you'll do? What time can we expect you back?—and then, crossing your fingers and saying a silent prayer, you let him go.

Your decision should flow from a feeling of mutual trust. If past performance gives you reason to believe that if you allow your child to stay by himself one weekend, a bacchanalia to end all others will result, then you are certainly within your rights to refuse. But if all you have to go on is a vague fear that *some*thing might happen if he doesn't go out to dinner with you on Friday, then you had better sit down and hold a high level summit meeting with yourself concerning your values about separation and independence.

There are no cut-and-dried rights and wrongs regarding separation and independence. What's proper for one child, in one family, in one community, may be improper for a similarly aged child in a neighboring town. It is important, too, to maintain faith in your own judgment and not be provoked by adolescent bravado. Parents, at times, do know best.

When Alex was 14, he told his father he wanted to go to a football game in a city sixty miles away. "Don't worry, Dad," he said. "I know all the trains and subways to take."

"I believe you," his father said. "But what would happen if a gang of older boys came up to you and demanded your gold chain?"

Alex proceeded to regale his father with a vivid description of how he and his friends would defend themselves manfully and courageously, with fists, knees, and whatever weapons happened to be handy.

Alex watched that game on television.

The next year when he again told his father he wanted to go to a baseball game, and his father asked the same question about the same gold chain, Alex said he wouldn't wear it.

He told his father all about the game when he returned.

There are effective ways and not-so-effective ways of checking an adolescent's judgment to make certain it is sound. Beware of taking too much pride in your teenager's independence at those times when it is unwarranted, but beware of stifling that independence in situations when only his pride or ego will be wounded if his judgment proves faulty. It's a tricky tightrope to walk, made even trickier by your own conflicting emotions as a parent who wants his child to be independent, yet at the same time feels a natural inclination to maintain the status quo.

Once again, we return to a message we've repeated: You know your child best. If you want clues as to how she'll handle issues of separation and independence in adolescence, look back at how she reacted in similar situations when she was 1, 2, 5 and 8 years old. The best indicator of future performance is past performance, and you can often find clues as to how an adolescent will handle the next stages by examining how she handled previous stages. So if you remember how your child acted in the past, you'll have an idea how she will react in the future—when she is getting ready to head to college, for instance.

Separation anxiety is common—on both sides—through-out the last two years of high school. More times than we care to count, calm, pleasant, easygoing twelfth graders have turned into adversarial, fight-provoking rebels. Although we do not condone this mode of behavior, we do understand its meaning: "I'm going to be leaving home soon, and it will be a difficult time for all of us, but if I can create havoc in the home before I leave, then we all will be happy when I go, and my departure will be less traumatic for everyone."

We've also seen longtime A and B students turn into juniors or seniors who suddenly manage no better than C's. Often, there is an important message behind that behavior: "I'm going to have to leave home soon, and I'm not sure I want to. I'm worried about the upcoming separation, so maybe if I don't do well I'll be able to delay it."

All students are apprehensive to some degree about going off to college. Parents are apprehensive, too. Try not to lose your sense of humor about this separation and independence issue. And difficult as this may sound, try not to be anxious. Trust the judgment and the actions of the adolescent you've been parenting for these many years. For nearly two decades now, you've been nurturing your child's independent streak, preparing her for the day she will take advantage of your work and become truly free.

Now it's about to happen. Instead of closing your eyes and fighting the inevitable flight, try instead to kick back, relax, and watch her soar. You've worked so long and hard to get your adolescent to this point. Let her independence be your reward, not your punishment. It's an exhilarating thing for her to experience—and it can be just as wonderful for you to see. After all, you got her there. Congratulations on a job well done.

12 | The Consequences of Not Saying No

Throughout this book, we have encouraged parents to say no to their teenagers creatively and positively. We have talked about how parents can say no to their adolescents' impulses and actions; how they can help their teenagers deal with those urges, and help them learn to say no themselves. We have also written about the necessity for parents to say no to their *own* impulses, and have suggested some strategies to enable them to do so.

We have noted that saying no means setting limits, both for parents and for adolescents, although we have stressed that those boundaries define an area inside of which plenty of "yeses" can be spoken. We have explained that "no" is not "never," nor is it negative or judgmental; rather, it is a loving limit that creates the positive space within which adolescents can test their hopes and dreams and explore their fears and anxieties.

We have done our best to describe "no" not as withholding, but as giving; not as an obstacle, but as an aid in ordering and structuring life as adolescents make their treacherous passage from dependence to independence. But we have not discussed the pitfalls, drawbacks, and consequences of not saying the dreaded "N" word. And what happens to those parents who *fail* to say no?

Parents who do not say no to their children teach a potentially dangerous lesson. One consequence of not saying no to adolescents whose impulses are a threat to themselves is that a form of anarchy occurs. It is an anarchy manifested by youngsters asking themselves (without saying so, of course), "Who's in charge here? What are the rules of this house?" In a family ruled by anarchy, there are no clearcut lines of authority. No one in the household understands who wields authority; even something as basic as the telephone becomes an anarchic symbol. In a family in which parents have failed to say no, the telephone may ring at inappropriate hours, night after night.

Ross was so unpopular as a 13-year-old that the phone never rang. Now, two years later, it rings constantly—during dinner, during the hours set aside for homework, sometimes even well beyond midnight. It is a welcome sound for his parents because it signifies their son's popularity and acceptance. So, rather than damage his newfound popularity, they hold their tongues and pull pillows over their ears. Their behavior is well-intentioned, but also very destructive. Ross (and his friends) receive the message that rules of civility and proper sleep habits are less important than gabbing on the phone. By sending that message, his parents make it difficult for him to understand that rules and regulations are more important than popularity.

Rebecca, 13 years old, has been assigned several age-appropriate chores, including folding the laundry. Every week she tends to put this off until the last possible second. Like many young teens, her popularity waxes and wanes; one night, just before laundry-folding time, she receives an invitation to go rollerblading with a new group of friends and out the door she heads. Another family member will have to fold the laundry. Dad volunteers, balancing his need for fresh shirts with his daughter's need to be accepted and feel part of a group.

By not saying no, Rebecca's parents have taught her the lesson that procrastination and avoidance work, and that social events can be placed before responsibility. Unfortunately, if Rebecca learns at 13 that she does not have to fold clothes when it is inconvenient, then at 15 she may believe that she does not have to obey a curfew if that too is inconvenient. And at 17, she may feel it's okay to take the family car for a spin in the wee hours of a school morning, simply because that is a convenient time to do so (and because her friends have asked her to). The anarchy of a 13-year-old may not be as obvious or grand as that of a 17-year-old—but the former often leads to the latter.

When parents do not say no, they fail to foster their teenagers' ability to order their own potentially harmful urges and impulses. When parents do not say no, they no longer reinforce the values that are so important to family life, and in fact run the risk of having a household without values (or in which the prevailing values change daily). And values are the system of continuity through which every man, woman, and child can live and grow together.

Like it or not, adolescence is a time of self-centeredness. And parents who fail to say no also fail to provide the starting block youngsters can push off from, as they move beyond their own self-centered adolescence into a well-defined, clearly-bounded adulthood, to become responsible, contributing citizens in their community and their world.

Kent grew up in a family with two college-educated parents. His father, Ben, was a middle-level manager in a large corporation; his mother, Gloria, returned to work in a retail store when Kent and his younger sister were in school full-time. Kent's doting and permissive grandfather "Pops" lived with the family since Kent was a child; in fact, he gave Ben and Gloria the down payment for their home, and within the family structure his opinion on most matters was given some weight. When Kent was in elementary school, he enjoyed a closer relationship with "Pops," particularly when they were able to share their common interests of fishing and baseball.

When Kent became 13 he turned moody. He seemed less available to his family, and in particular disappointed his grandfather by failing to show up for fishing dates and baseball games the older man had looked forward to. He was marginally testing rules, but his parents never said "no" to his behavior; they never forced him to take responsibility for his actions.

Reports began to filter home from school: Kent was cutting classes, fighting, acting rudely to teachers. At home he was "stretching" curfews, then missing them altogether. His limit-testing was becoming more and more obvious, but "boys will be boys" became his parents' unspoken motto. They didn't say it, exactly, but their lack of action conveyed that message.

Then family friends began telling Ben and Gloria that Kent had been seen with young people from surrounding towns whose reputations were suspect. The youth leader at church mentioned to Gloria that Kent seemed "disengaged" and apathetic toward the youth group that had previously been very important to him. His attendance was sporadic, the youth leader said—surprising news to his parents, since he often told them that's where he was headed.

Ben and Gloria attempted to initiate several talks with Kent, about different situations and in various settings, but they all ended up the same. Their overtures ended with Kent storming off, shouting insults. Each time his parents consoled themselves by saying, "It's just a phase. He'll grow out of it." But by not saying no to Kent's irresponsible behavior, they did nothing to help Kent realize he had to take definite responsibility for his own actions.

There was a steady, downward progression to Kent's behavior. At 15, Kent always seemed in the forefront of confrontations with authority figures, inside and outside of school. Having grown into an athletic, muscular young man, he looked for chances to fight. He became more verbally abusive at home, and although he never actually raised his hand against his mother, she became aware of an implied sense of threat.

Even his grandfather's entreaties were turned aside. The time they spent together shrank to a few minutes each week. Still, despite the many warning signs, Ben and Gloria clung to the hope that Kent's behavior was "just a phase."

They even said it was "just a phase" late one night when they found Kent—and the car—gone at 2 A.M. When they confronted him the next morning a major fight erupted; Kent once again turned his back on them, and stalked out the door.

Kent's parents moved from bafflement to paralysis. They had no idea what action—if any—to take. Embarrassed by the disorder in their home, they immersed themselves in their jobs. They could not bring themselves to talk about their problem—Kent's problem—with others, nor could they seek help within the community. Pops, saddened and distressed by the situation in the once-happy home, moved into a retirement community.

Although Kent's behavior had clearly become more provocative, challenging, and rebellious, no one close to him seemed able to act in an effective way, to change his behavior or even address the problem. His parents continued in their failure to acknowledge the gravity of the situation, still hoping (even after several years) that it would vanish.

Of course, it did not. At 17, Kent was well known to the town's youth officer, who regularly questioned him about destruction of mailboxes, driving on golf courses, and similar incidents.

A physically attractive youngster, Kent's late night outings often involved conquests of younger girls. He was unable to sustain a dating relationship with females his own age, and gained the nickname "E.G." among his friends, which stood for "eighth grade," the girls he loved to boast about.

He was involved in a major accident, and though the word was that he had been drinking, he was not given a sobriety test because the crash occurred at midday. His parents hired an attorney to make sure that Kent's rights were protected and did not ask Kent to reimburse them for legal fees. They didn't feel that would be right; after all, he was having such difficulty holding a job.

At the same time his school attendance and participation became marginal. With no parent at home, he spent a good portion of each day sleeping. The rest of the time he was awake and in charge of "Party Central" (as the house became known to his friends). Ben and Gloria remained perplexed, confused, and frustrated—still hoping that Kent would "grow up and come to his senses."

Finally Kent was arrested for selling drugs inside his school. Although he protested (as always) that he was innocent ("I was just keeping them for someone"), he was assigned to a probation officer and social worker. In the course of the family study, the social worker discovered the long-standing lack of responsible limit-setting behavior by Kent's parents. Throughout adolescence—even earlier—Ben and Gloria had not given Kent the boundaries, structure, order, and consequences he so desperately needed, thereby significantly interfering with his ability to develop responsible behavior controls.

Turning away from the problem, hoping that time would heal and bring change, *they* became the problem. Rather than let Kent learn that he was responsible for his own behavior, *they* became responsible for it. The results were plain, and painful to see.

The shock of finally having boundaries was good for Kent. On the court's recommendation, the entire family went into treatment. Working with a counselor, each member came to see his or her role more clearly defined. Ben and Gloria needed the support of the community in order to become more "parental," and Kent needed his parents' support in order to become less destructive. It was not easy, but with the support of each other, the household eventually became a much more comfortable place to be.

Not all such stories end so happily. Some adolescents whose parents do not say no never get the chance to have limits placed on their behavior. They never have the opportunity to learn that there is a distinction between what they *want* to do and what they *may* do. The results can be seen every day in the way such undisciplined individuals conduct their dangerous or limited lives.

Of course, parents who *do* say no suffer consequences, too. When they place limits on behavior, their adolescent may become angry with them. They may want to be seen as their teenager's "friend" or "ally" during this difficult transition phase, and saying no is not a surefire way to be thought of (at least at this stage) as a buddy. Parents may feel they have ceased to be a valued part of their child's life; they might even worry that they will lose the affection and love of their adolescent.

But parents should recognize this fear for what it is, and then look beyond it. They must have faith that the values they have been communicating since their teenager was a baby have not only been heard, but also incorporated. Parents need to believe that the current stormy relationship will survive and emerge strong and firm after the adolescent hurricane has passed. And they must believe, especially, that the chances of this happening are lessened if they do not say no.

Parents are not, after all, saying no to their adolescents; they are saying no simply to their *impulses*, which they are incapable of controlling by themselves. It is not the parent, but rather the impulse—the urge or feeling—that makes adolescents angry, and when the impulse period passes, they will be thankful or appreciative that their parents stood there strongly for them when they needed them most—even if they didn't realize it at the time.

The positive consequences of saying no far outweigh the negative ones. As we've noted throughout this book, saying no helps adolescents define a situation, and in so doing enables them to define their separate identity. It assists them in discharging their impulses in an orderly, appropriate manner; to become responsible citizens; to be his or her own human being.

Saying no to some things means saying yes to others. Parents must pick and choose their spots and avoid the trap of arbitrary, autocratic nay-saying. "No" need not be an inhibiting, constricting word; it should be a freeing, emancipating action.

George was a teacher. After his wife's untimely death (when his children Reed and Cheryl were 8 and 6), George became the actual and spiritual father and mother to them both. This responsibility was important to him; he was determined to make up for the loss his children had experienced.

George said no to certain, dangerous impulses his children had, but in other instances where no danger was involved he said yes, and let them seek their own identities while making their own mistakes. And then he said no again, to his own impulse to stifle his adolescents' desires to live their own lives as they wanted to, once they began to discover who they were and could define their own expectations and aspirations.

His marriage three years after his wife's death to Vanessa, a florist, provided Reed and Cheryl with a good friend. The children called her by her first name, and she worked hard to keep the memory of their mother alive in the house. Together, George and Vanessa continued the responsibility of parenting he had worked at so assiduously with his first wife.

When Reed was 14, a young neighbor gave him a motorbike. Though the bike was clearly fun and coveted, ownership was against the law. And despite Reed's strong pleadings (and George's internal questioning), George insisted that Reed return the bike. He said it was illegal, and too dangerous, for a 14-year-old to ride such a vehicle on the streets of town.

For some time after that Reed was sullen and angry. More than once George second-guessed his decision, but he remained steadfast. And Vanessa, as always, was supportive.

When Reed turned 17, he bought a dirt bike with his earnings from a summer job. George still thought it was dangerous, but he felt more secure that Reed could handle the risk. Eventually, the two of them were able to look back on the memory of "the motorbike incident" with less bitterness, more understanding, even a touch of humor.

Meanwhile, when Cheryl was 13 and showing promise as violinist, she decided she did not want to play. She balked at practicing and created an enormous furor over lessons. Music had been an important part of George's relationship with his first wife, and it was only with great difficulty that he came to the decision not to struggle with Cheryl over this issue. He allowed her to stop, and she did so with glee.

Then at 16 she became enamored of a trumpet player —and the trumpet. George and Vanessa agreed that the decision made when Cheryl was a 13-year-old could be altered for a 16-year-old, and they agreed to pay for lessons. They realized they could not force their expectations on Cheryl when she was 13, and struggling to develop her own aspirations and values. They also realized that at 16 she was still developing and changing, and they could help her fulfill the promise and interest (in this case, in music) she could not recognize at 13.

Interestingly, as Reed grew older and entered his junior year in college, he tossed aside his previous thoughts of being a professional motorcycle racer or an automotive design engineer, and announced plans to become a photographer. Cheryl, an excellent student with high SATs, decided to attend music school, rather than George's Ivy League alma mater.

George accepted those decisions. He understood that a parent is not an adolescent's best friend, a stern authority figure, or a detached "counselor" type; not a punisher, a pal, prisoner, or a patsy. A parent is, quite simply and basically, a *parent*. A parent of an adolescent, but a parent nonetheless.

As a parent, you must always remain true to yourself—and it is impossible to be true if you are busy being your kid's best buddy. Know and respect the moat that separates the adult and adolescent worlds; be friendly, but don't be friends. Throughout their lives, your children will have shiploads of friends, but they'll never have another set of parents. Once those boundaries have been crossed (and this can only happen if the parent acquiesces, either tacitly or expressly), then your ability to act as a parent, to send messages, to set values, to observe as a much-needed role model, is temporarily diminished, if not irrevocably destroyed.

What's the difference between being friendly and acting like a best friend? It's the difference between dropping your daughter off at a rock concert and returning later to pick her up, or sitting in the seat next to her as if you're 15 again; it's the difference between taking your son to the movies, or renting a "XXX" video for him and his friends.

Your aim as a parent of an adolescent should be not to control your adolescent's behavior but rather to help your adolescent learn to control his or her own behavior. There will be moments when you may need to step in, to help your adolescent order certain behavior, but this should be a rare occurrence, not a matter of course.

How do you do it? There is no single right answer, no button you can push to send yourself into Automatic Parent Pilot mode. The task is far tougher than that; it calls for you to use your own judgment over and over again in the ongoing process of drawing fine lines in the shifting sands of family relationships. And you must continually check yourself, to examine whether you're keeping yourself on the parental side of that line.

If you fail to accomplish all that today, don't worry. Regroup; retrench; reassess. There's apt to be a new challenge fifteen minutes from now. Prepare for it; embrace it; relish it, for it is a challenge for which you have been preparing for over a decade, and it is a challenge you are well equipped to meet.

It must be obvious by now that this book is not a cookbook of answers to specific issues. Rather, it is a guide to help you handle the tumultuous events of adolescence—some awesome, others niggling; some heart-stopping, others laughable—and to handle them from a family perspective. It is a challenge to you (and your spouse or significant other) to examine your values, so that you can be better prepared to share those values with your adolescent.

Your values pervade every aspect of your life, from how often you attend church, to how fast you drive, to whether or not you enjoy dining at expensive restaurants. Values help define your religious, business, social, and recreational lives, as well as your family life. And every family's value system is unique. That's why this book must be a guide, not a blueprint. There are no perfect families, just as there are no perfect children—or parents. Thus there can be no perfect answers. What there can be, however, is a compassionate, value-filled way of thinking and living with one another, based upon honest, open lines of communication.

If we send clear, truthful messages to our children, and if we interpret what they are saying to us realistically and nonjudgmentally, then we can build trust with them. And at the same time, we'll truly begin to trust ourselves.

Never forget that you're the only parent your children will ever have. They can't fire you, divorce you, or trade you in for a sleeker, snazzier parental model. You're secure in that title, even if you feel insecure in that role. But neither can you fire, divorce, or trade in your children for new, improved versions. And that is simply all the more reason to remain constant in your own values, and to feel confident that adolescent fads, mood swings, experiments and mating games are all just tests, for you and for your child.

So: Resist that temptation to relate to your teenager as a friend or a pal. Remain a parent. And as your adolescent develops and matures, she'll steadily grow into a person in her own right. At that point, almost without realizing it, you'll discover a newfound closeness you yearned for earlier. You'll enjoy a unique relationship with a separate, decent human being whom you helped create, and then allowed to create herself.

You'll still be a parent, but you'll be embarking on another exciting phase of parenthood.

13 | **F**inding the Courage to Find Help

Throughout the past twelve chapters we have indicated, through specific examples and general concepts, some of the joys and perplexities of being a parent of an adolescent. We hope that many of the case studies we have presented will hold some meaning for you and your family. With perseverance and a bit of luck, perhaps the "solutions" to some of our examples will square precisely with the dilemmas you face—but that may not always be the case. Sometimes a family's earnest search for answers will hit a dead end. The problems will loom too large; the family will be unable to find solutions without help.

But what does that mean? What kind of help? Where do you go to find it? And how do you know if the help you get is effective?

Sarah and her family needed help. She began her scholastic career in a place that encouraged creativity and independence, but when she was in fifth grade her parents felt that the school was too "open-ended" and placed her in a more traditional setting. She squeaked through middle school, but when she reached the local high school, her grades began to plummet.

Every night after dinner she would retreat to her room, pull the shades and play heavy metal albums (she especially liked the sounds of dissonance and discord). She took the car out once at two in the morning, and disappeared for three days.

When she returned she agreed (reluctantly) to see a therapist, but it proved to be a terrible match. Her therapist wanted to take walks by the brook and talk quietly, but Sarah was too active and inarticulate for that. When she told her parents that the therapy was not working, they interpreted it as resistance—to the therapist and to their own attempt to solve a problem—and forced her to continue ("if you expect to live in this house").

But after four months of weekly tugs-of-war, Sarah's mother was talking with a neighbor, and during the conversation heard the name of another therapist she'd met once at a party. She recalled how impressed she'd been with her, and asked Sarah if she wanted to switch.

Almost immediately, things got better. Sarah related to her new therapist the moment they met ("She even knows the groups I listen to!" she said after the first session), and she appreciated for the first time that her parents were truly trying to help her. Soon, at the therapist's urging, Sarah and her father began their first project together: building a guitar from scratch. It took a long time, and there were some tense moments along the way. There were also some very funny times, and after a few months Sarah and her father had completed an instrument of which they both were quite proud.

It took some guts for Sarah's parents to realize that the original "match" was not a good one, and take charge of the situation to change it. But they did, and the story had a happy ending. Sarah finished high school, was accepted at college—and before leaving that fall, she wrote both her therapist and her parents long, appreciative letters.

Dennis also needed help. For as long as anyone could remember, he had been everyone's friend: always smiling, joking, lending a supportive hand or ear. But beginning in ninth grade his grades began to slide, and despite his howls of protest (his social life had continued to flourish) his parents sent him to parochial school.

Halfway through the first semester of eleventh grade, Dennis stole some money from the school store. When confronted, he first denied any wrongdoing, but he then admitted to it. He was asked to leave the school. Though his parents, teachers, and counselors pressed him for a reason why he had taken the money, he never gave one. Everyone was perplexed; he had a regular allowance, and plenty of money in his bank account.

One night shortly after going back to public school, Dennis went into the bathroom and ingested an entire bottle of aspirin. He didn't tell his parents—but he panicked, made himself vomit, then walked into their bedroom and asked if he could "see someone about a problem."

That grabbed Dennis' parents' attention as nothing before had. They became sensitive to his needs and stood by his side the rest of the school year, which he spent at home. They entered a family treatment program with him, and by the end of that spring they were feeling as good about Dennis as he was feeling about himself.

His sliding grades had been Dennis' first cries for help; taking the money was his second. Swallowing the aspirin, was of course, his third and most desperate cry.

The point here is that adolescents cannot always ask for what they need. Instead they may throw out dramatic, dangerous signals—and if one does not work, they will try another. Dennis had to try three times before his parents heard his cries. When they did, they realized how significant those cries were, and they acted quickly. They got Dennis the help he was so desperately asking for.

Bart, too, needed help. An inveterate "thrill freak," his search for adventure intensified when Bart hit adolescence. He began smoking cigarettes, then pot; he started hanging around with older boys and girls; he defined "the edge" on which some people live life.

Bart was an energetic, athletic boy, but he never tried out for any teams. Skateboarding, hotdog skiing, high diving— any sport that carried a risk and demanded that his body be pushed to the limit appealed to him. Although he was often injured, he continued to take chances—except during his "melancholy" periods, when he withdrew by himself into a world of drugs and alcohol. As he entered his mid-teens, those periods occurred with greater and greater frequency.

The pattern of hyperactivity, followed by bouts of drinking and drugs, intensified during high school. His parents attributed it to their son's basic temperament ("Barton was born that way," they'd sigh). Sometimes they pretended that such behavior was almost normal, colluding in their denial of the problem.

Bart made it to college (he was not a poor student, although his behavior gave most of his teachers fits), and only when his substance abuse became so dramatic that he was asked to leave did his parents realize he had both a drug and psychological problem demanding dramatic intervention. His parents placed him in a treatment facility with programs to address both substance abuse and mental health problems, and over a long period of time, Bart got better.

WHERE TO GO

So we're back to the question we asked at the beginning of this chapter: Where do you go for help?

The first group of helpers may be called "gatekeepers." They provide the initial entrance into the world of treatment for problems that have grown too great for a family to solve by itself. Included among these "gatekeepers" are school personnel (guidance counselors, psychologists, social workers, even trusted teachers and coaches), doctors (pediatricians and family practitioners), clergy, and youth workers.

These "gatekeepers" serve as impartial third parties. They allow you to unburden your worries and fears; they can assure you that you are not a "bad" or "failed" parent, and they can point you in the direction of other therapists able to provide more intensive, long-term treatment. The "gatekeepers" can help lead you through the maze of referral resources; they know who in your community are experts in dealing with adolescents and their families: mental health professionals, psychiatrists, psychologists, social workers, marriage and family counselors, and trained clergy.

It's certainly all right to ask for referrals from friends and people you know who have had similar problems in the past. It's also perfectly all right today to be a "wise consumer." If you feel secure and comfortable with the first professional you talk to, great; if you don't, then interview others. A therapist may have a Rolodex filled with satisfied patients and may be admired by masses, but there may be many reasons (such as gender, age, interests, and personality) why that therapist may not be right for you. If you sense "fit" is poor—during an initial meeting, or after a reasonable amount of time—then do not hesitate to seek a change.

It is important when you seek help that you find a person who will help you support your own values. You must feel comfortable with an individual who understands the behavior of your adolescent; who understands that this behavior has meaning; and who seems to support the family values that you have established. The therapist's job is to help you express those values better, or to reformulate them in a way that will be more productive for your adolescent. You must thus feel confident that you and the man or woman you choose to work with understands those values.

What happens if your adolescent absolutely, positively, no-two-ways-about-it refuses to go to a professional?

Then *you* can go. There's nothing wrong—in fact, there are many things right—with you going to a therapist yourself. You can talk to your therapist about ways of engaging your adolescent in the process of change, or about ways of functioning around that youngster's aversion to therapy.

You can be supported by your therapist—and many times a change in one person in a family can affect everyone else in that family. A youngster who sees a parent affect change in his or her life may choose to get involved with a professional later, in order to change his or her own life. And if your adolescent needs a significant change—moving to a group home or hospitalization, for instance—then your sessions with a trained professional might help you bring about that change in your adolescent.

Seeking professional help is not an easy step to take. It takes courage to admit that things are awry, and that outside assistance is needed. But it is a vital step to take—and it is a step that will lead you out of the thicket of family problems, onto the path toward happier family relations.

Epilogue

A suggestion to consider: Every family might well consider an annual "mental health checkup" with a trained mental health professional. This is simply a session attended by the entire family, at which all family members discuss issues of mutual concern, clear the air, and reestablish communication under the direction of a practitioner who does this sort of thing all the time.

The Recker family have decided to have a mental health checkup one year, and it has worked wonders. They are a fairly typical middle class, suburban family. Bob Recker, an executive with a large corporation, has been transferred every few years by his company. He travels considerably; in fact, he is absent from home so often that a dinner appearance becomes an event worth remarking upon. "Dad, you're home!" one of the youngsters inevitably says. "What's the matter?"

Two years ago Beth Recker returned to work full-time in an art supply store, after spending several years doing volunteer work in the community. She and her husband are graduates of the same college; they met during freshman orientation. They are devoted to their alma mater, attending football games with old friends, and wearing college sweatshirts.

Sally, an eleventh grader, and Doug, in ninth grade, both have the potential to do well in school, but their grades are as variable as their behavior. They never make the "Police Reports" section of the local paper—but they're never far away from it. Although Beth was a "jock" in college (she was a standout swimmer) and Bob played in the most well-known rock group on campus, neither of their children seems interested in music or sports. Sally and Doug were given piano lessons when they were younger, but soon pestered their parents into letting them quit. Beth was president of the Little League and coached both children's travel soccer teams, but by middle school neither Sally nor Doug was interested in organized athletics.

Sally seems very involved in environmental issues and often lectures her parents on their wasteful habits. She works weekends (and one night a week) at an ice cream store and is also interested in poetry. Doug's friends are heavy metallers; when they're not listening to music, they like to play "hacky sack." Bob and Beth Recker say very little about any of those activities—environmentalism, poetry, music and hacky sack—which the youngsters interpret as disapproval.

The family is intact, but not happy. Daily life is a series of conflicts: over chores, room conditions, friends, summer plans. Contact between any two members of the family is limited to a few words, and both Sally and Doug spend most of their time either in their rooms or "out."

Last spring Carol, Beth's colleague at work, suggested the family go for a "mental health checkup." She recommended a counselor who had given a similar "checkup" to her family. Bob was noncommittal when she mentioned it to him; he'd go, he said, but he doubted the kids would, and then what good would that do?

Sally and Doug were opposed to the idea. Coordinating schedules would be next to impossible, they said. When Beth told them about the experience of Carol's family, and since Sally and Doug liked Carol's teenagers, they agreed to give it a try.

The Reckers spent an hour with the therapist one Wednesday evening, and though they couldn't put their finger on any one thing she said or did, they agreed it had been a worthwhile session. She pointed out things they hadn't thought of before; they discussed issues they had not realized had been bothering them, and they did it in a low-key, nonconfrontational setting. They left her office in high spirits, and then went for a snack at the store where Sally worked. When Doug mentioned it was the first time they had all been there at once, they laughed together.

As youngsters move from one stage of development to the next, parents often do not adjust their expectations of their adolescents accordingly—nor do adolescents adjust their expectations of their parents. The entire family becomes fixed at a point that's inappropriate for the teenagers' developmental stages.

A "mental health checkup" can bring a family together when it hits that point, just as it did for the Recker family. Through such a session, once a year, family members can rediscover the ties that bind them together, can readjust the intricate threads of their relationships—and can move on to the next stage in life, which is after all, a series of rewarding, exciting next stages.

Index